D0898239

THE BOYS
ON THE PORCH

An Allegory: Bridges from Fear to Faith

June Eastvold

Other books by June Eastvold:

Read My Tail:
Testimony of a Terrier Named Brandy

Another 2nd Chance:
Poetry and Photography by June Eastvold

THE BOYS
ON THE PORCH

An Allegory: Bridges from Fear to Faith

JUNE NILSSEN EASTVOLD

Henschel
HAUS
publishing, inc.
MILWAUKEE WISCONSIN

Copyright © 2014 by June Nilssen Eastvold
All rights reserved.

Published by
HenschelHAUS Publishing, Inc.
www.HenschelHAUSbooks.com

Paperback ISBN: 978159598-338-1
Hardcover ISBN: 978159598-371-8
E-ISBN: 978159598-339-8
LCCN: 2014946066

Publisher's Cataloging-In-Publication Data
(Prepared by The Donohue Group, Inc.)

Eastvold, June Nilssen.
The boys on the porch : an allegory : bridging faith and fear / June
Nilssen Eastvold.

pages : illustrations ; cm

Issued also as an ebook.
ISBN: 978-1-59598-338-1

1. Homeless men--Fiction. 2. Middle class--Fiction.
3. Material culture--Religious aspects--Christianity--Fiction. 4.
Neighborliness--Fiction. 5. Christian life--Fiction. 6. Seattle (Wash.)--
Fiction. 7. Allegories. 8. Christian fiction. I. Title.

PS3605.A88 B69 2014
813/.6   2014946066

Cover design by Kevin Gardner.

This book is dedicated to my husband,
MICHAEL FROME,
whose inspiration and persistent
encouragement challenged me
to write this story.

TABLE OF CONTENTS

Foreword... i

Preface... iii

Introduction v

1. The Neighbors & the Bishop 1

2. Who is Our Neighbor? 11

3. Midnight on the Porch 15

4. The Bridge 21

5. City Center... 33

6. Here I Stand... 49

7. Loose 53

8. Pros and Cons...................................... 71

9. For Everything There is a Season.......... 77

10. The Letter.. 87

11. Patrick 99

12. Easter 113

13. Mother's Day 129

14. "Lord, To Whom Shall We Go?" 139

15. The Upper Room.................................. 163

16. The Runaways..................................... 173

17. Amazing Grace 187

Afterword 195

Discussion Questions................................ 199

Acknowledgments 201

About the Author 203

FOREWORD

The Boys on the Porch, written with a poetic flare by a retired Evangelical Lutheran Church in America pastor, June Nilssen Eastvold, is a compelling story because it is a true story. And it is compelling because it is written by the person who was at the center of the stormy drama that involved her congregation, the home owners and business people near their sanctuary—and "the boys on the porch."

It's a drama that took place in the early 1990s in Seattle, Washington. But it's a drama that is being repeated, with different twists and turns in the story line, in every city, and even in small towns, of this country.

This is a volume that will hold the interest of any reader who enjoys a story that is the stuff of real-life passions, struggles, surprises, successes, failures, and mysteries. It will have a deeper attraction for those who want to grapple with the enigmas of homelessness, alcoholism, and potential solutions. And it will have an even deeper attraction for those who want to grapple with the call of faith—and for Christians, the call of the Gospel—to discern what decisions to make, as the culture pulls in the direction of a comfortable, economically advantageous lifestyle, the congregational tradition pulls in the direction of life together without struggle or controversy—and the Gospel speaks of a radical love of God and neighbor that trumps the world's culture and the congregational tradition.

The literary world, the religious community, and all those working for the common good of all, owe much to June Nilssen Eastvold for taking this dramatic story, after twenty years, off the shelf, and getting it to the publisher.

Rev. Joseph W. Ellwanger
Retired ELCA Pastor
Author of *Strength for the Struggle:
Insights from the Civil Rights Movement
and Urban Ministry*

"The Lord our God is one;
and you shall love the Lord your God
with all your heart, and with all your soul
and with all your mind, and with all your strength."

The second is this:
"You shall love your neighbor as yourself."

There are no other commandments
greater than these.

—Mark 12: 30-31

PREFACE

For over twenty years, this manuscript has been on and off my shelf. Within those years, I have encountered the homeless in many cities—living under bridges, sleeping in doorways, lining up at food pantries or soup kitchens, or frequenting church offices in quest of assistance. I have seen the flight of refugees, seeking asylum, shelter, food, and safely.

With each review of this story, I have discovered it to be an allegory, defined as the veiled presentation, in a figurative story, of a meaning metaphorically implied, but not expressly stated.

It is my hope that you, the reader, will move between virtual reality to stories of the imagination that reveal hope, humor, and deep emotional feeling ...

As the boys say, in their flights of fantasy and the sharing of their stories with others, they find common ground and acceptance.

Hope is not possible without the help and the collaboration of a loving community.

We do not transcend or deny suffering or despair. We walk up the steps in the dark of midnight, open to meeting the strangers who have appeared in our "place." It will take a long time, but we will be better for it.

NOTE:
While based on actual happenings,
names, dialogues, and certain
characters have been added and
altered.

—June Nilssen Eastvold

INTRODUCTION

They defecated in the bushes, urinated and puked on the sidewalk, spit blood, and sometimes even died. Nobody invited them. Few expected them to stay. But they did. And days lengthened into years.

In the early 1990s, after drifting through Seattle's streets, the boys on the porch established their headquarters at University Lutheran Church. They discovered a place—our place. The entrance covered them from the rain without closing them in from the sky and the trees. The church was a sanctuary where they were protected from the law and the young gangs that robbed and beat them in the dark alleys before dawn. They stared at the stars, told stories from the foxholes in Vietnam, sucked their wine bottles to the bottom, and rolled down the hill to panhandle early in the morning.

Since I am Pastor June, the teller of the tales, let me start by setting the scene and introducing myself.

The church building is situated on a busy corner near the campus of the University of Washington, in a residential Seattle neighborhood up the hill a few blocks east of University Avenue where the business area in the University District is centered. Fraternity and sorority houses line the boulevard further up the hill beyond the church and homeowners pride themselves on their well-kept houses, yards, and gardens on our block. The congregation is composed of primarily white, educated professionals who consider themselves to be progressive thinkers.

On a clear, late afternoon, standing outside the church at the top of 50th, I saw the Olympic Mountains to the west. An unbroken string of red taillights blinked like Christmas bulbs looking for the evergreens that disappeared long ago. The evening rush hour traffic linked bumper to bumper on the crowded freeway stretched out beyond and below me.

The city is no longer a fishing, logging pioneer town. You have to sign up for a tour now to re-visit the legends of historic characters, expeditions, brothels, and prospectors.

Built on seven hills, surrounded by mountains, Seattle is linked together with bridges and ship canals that connect to Puget Sound. The city is crowded, the possibilities for expansion limited. Housing for the poor has been replaced with pricey condos and high-rise office buildings. It is still the city that fuels the great American dream, drawing prospectors to the west to strike it rich in Bill Gate's gold rush.

It takes money to buy living space in Seattle. Houses themselves are gold mines these days. Nobody wants another useless mouth to feed, or drunks decorating the curbs, or tramps begging at the kitchen door.

Certainly not in our neighborhood.

At one time, University Lutheran was a little chapel on the green. It was a favorite place for weddings, so popular it began to grow, and like many congregations after World War II, the boom called for classrooms, a larger sanctuary, and a diversified outreach. The location and the building became a source of pride, priority, and investment of time and finances. Homes around it had equal commitment to protect the character and quality of the area.

I was told that just before I came, a conflict arose around remodeling the chancel in the church sanctuary. Bitter differences between my predecessor and an influential leader in the congregation focused around re-designing "sacred space."

Change. Invasion of tradition. Differences in understanding of liturgical uses. Taking stands in the interest of preserving the integrity of Lutheran theology. All of this came down to an internal power struggle between the pastor and the millionaire contributor who sustained the budget each year.

At last, when reason prevailed, the battles quieted down, and a compromise plan was adopted. But not without a price. The stress took a toll on my predecessor's health, causing him to step over into medical care and retirement. In the interest of healing divisions within the membership, an Interim Pastor was assigned to reconcile the differences and build a bridge to the future.

No one was anxious to spark another fire.

They took a chance on me. I was in my late fifties, recently divorced, and from the Midwest. I became of interest to them because I had been on the Commission of Seventy elected to bring together major Lutheran bodies into one Evangelical Lutheran Church in America. I was among the first women to be ordained, and had experience serving in academic settings.

My first call was to Fourth Lutheran at the foot of the campus of Wittenberg University and Hamma School of Theology in Springfield, Ohio, where most of the members of the congregation were on faculties or students; and as Campus Pastor at the University of Wisconsin–Milwaukee, where I founded the Gamaliel Chair, a program for Peace and Justice.

From there, I became the Senior Pastor at a once prestigious congregation on the south side of the city of Milwaukee that had been swept along by dramatic urban changes. I headed a male multi-racial staff, was called to lead a tri-lingual body of

Hmong, Hispanic, and the heirs of Norwegian immigrants who had started the church over 100 years before.

I looked impressive on paper, and our interviews went well. Still, it was a bold move in 1990 to call a woman. The old-timers admitted they had serious reservations. I took a big leap, too. I sold my house, gave away most of my household belongings, and came alone to the West Coast, leaving my family, my only grandchild, and treasured friends behind. After fifteen years, I had built a strong network in Milwaukee.

But I wanted one more frontier, one more challenge. I got it.

Chapter One

THE NEIGHBORS
AND THE BISHOP

A s I was looking out the window from my Hobbit Hole, gazing at the skies over the ship canal below, Emily stood at her kitchen window, at the end of the block where the church stood, debating the same question I was. We had never met, yet we held in common the same sky above us. Our question: *Was it going to rain?*

Still new to the coast, I decided to take my umbrella. Emily decided to take the dog out for her morning jaunt, expecting only light coastal mist.

Petunia, her adorable, fluffy, white pedigreed poodle, was waiting at the front door. Together they greeted the overcast morning, filled with good cheer and a snappy step. Emily always looked for the sun to crack through as the day developed. The very early hours of day were cool and refreshing. The line of houses along the street still had drawn shades and no signs of awakening. It was as though they had the neighborhood to themselves, quiet and at rest.

About two miles away, at the foot of Capitol Hill, I stepped into the shower, reviewing what was on my agenda for the day at church. The coffee was perking in the kitchen, Bach was flowing from the classical station on the radio, and I was luxuriating in suds and hot water. I had treated myself to new towels when I moved into my new place. Big towels that I could wrap around myself. Soft, comforting, embracing! AH!

Meanwhile, Emily and Petunia advanced on their walk, pausing here and there for a sniff at some favorite bushes and a squat to poop on Tim and Sadie's lawn. Emily, afraid they might be looking from behind their drapes, always made a conscious effort to carefully clean up. It was what a good neighbor was responsible to do.

This particular morning, however, something was different. As they approached the church on the corner, Petunia started to bark. She strained to get loose from her leash, almost tipping Emily over on the sidewalk. Above her barking, a strange noise sounded from the church porch. Snores? Camel humps lined up in a row at the tops of the steps. As Emily tried to control Petunia, she also tried to control her own disbelief and shock.

Suddenly, a red-faced, bearded man sat up and shouted at her, "What the hell? Can't a man get a decent night's sleep anymore? Shut up, you pampered, pimpy, toy mutt. Get your legs trimmed! Son-of-a-bitch. Leave us alone!"

Then the face disappeared again under his hump, while other humps began to move about and threatened to appear.

Emily pulled Petunia around and they hurriedly retreated back down to the other end of the block. She would definitely report this to the police, notify the daycare and send out an alarm to all the neighbors.

This was an outrage!

Emily lost no time. The afternoon of her encounter, she appeared in my office with two other neighbors to file a protest against

the boys on the porch. The delegation repre-
sented "my kind": middle-class, white,
educated people who know how to pick up
the phone, network, and exert influence in
important places.

I had never met any of them before. I
learned that Emily owned a house at the
other end of the block. She was a divorced,
professional woman who rented rooms to
select university students to make additional
income to pay expenses. Her house was her
castle.

She was accompanied by an attorney
who lived directly across the alley from her.
He showed me a picture of his seven-year-old
daughter, an adorable child with bright red
hair and sparkling blue eyes. Only two years
before, a bumbling, big-bellied vagrant had
confronted her in their backyard, causing her
to run screaming into the kitchen, terrified.
Her mother called the police and since that
incident, they never allowed the girl to play
alone outside. It was obvious that the men on
the porch were making him paranoid.

The third member of the delegation was a
professor who taught at the university. He

was a mild-mannered fellow who seemed to have come along out of loyalty to the others.

I was not unsympathetic to their complaints. As the mother of three and a devoted grandmother, I could feel the weight of the father's anxiety about the safety of his lovely young daughter. I also knew how tough divorce is and what a challenge it is to protect one's investments as a single woman. I wanted to like them. If I recognized having met the men on the porch before, I also recognized how many times I had faced these people before.

I listened intently, offered them coffee, and tried to measure their body language, as well as our conversation. Apparently I communicated the wrong message because they each shook my hand cordially as Emily said with great satisfaction, "WONDERFUL! So it's all taken care of then."

"Let's just say that we will continue to discuss the matter," I replied as I escorted them out of my office.

When they had gone I stood with my back against the door, wondering if this question of mercy and fairness is ever "all taken care of, then."

The church council was scheduled to meet that evening. I began to focus my mind on how to introduce the situation so that the men, as well as the neighbors, could get a fair hearing. To defend the homeless in this context would be a tough assignment. All the cards were stacked against the men. I tried to think of at least one story where Jesus stood against the outcasts and I couldn't come up with one.

Emily wasn't the only one who contacted the Bishop. After a series of calls, he determined that he should invite me to come to his office to discuss the matter.

It was mid-morning, a week after Emily's encounter with one of the boys on the porch. When I walked into the Bishop's office, he greeted me with a cordial handshake.

"I have a pot of hot coffee here and a cinnamon roll, fresh baked from our kitchen oven. I brought it from the breakfast table. Enjoy!"

"Good start, anyway," I thought.

He went on. "I suppose you know why I asked you to come in to talk with me."

"I am guessing it is about the men who are staying on our front porch at the church."

"They've put me under a lot of pressure", he laughed. "The *Seattle Times* religion editor has picked up the trail and seems to think there is a real story here. I have even been advised to use my authority to discipline you."

"You certainly have the right to do that," I answered.

"The right to do what?" he responded calmly.

"To enforce your authority. Lots of people are upset."

" I think I have heard from all of them. Now, I want to hear from you."

I hesitated. What should I say? I decided to say what I honestly thought.

"Well, I think these men have been sent to us. I think they are angels on our doorstep, visitors appearing with a purpose. The church is their sanctuary, a meeting ground, a Light on the hill. I believe, in time, we will recognize who they are and why they are present with us ..."

He paused, thinking about what I had just said. I appreciated that.

Then, he continued. "I have been giving this considerable thought. If I were a judge, I would be forced to respond according to the law. Calls have been coming from people demanding that I order immediate action to remove these men from the church property. Let me read you the list of complaints. They raise questions of public health; defamation of property; disturbance of the peace; disrespect for neighbors; fear for the safety of children in the daycare center in the church basement; decline in property values; impact on business down the Ave.

"These calls are from people in the neighborhood, the university, the Chamber of Commerce, real estate agents, health administrators, even the mayor's office. Members of your congregation, other pastors in the area..." He stopped and looked straight at me.

"I have been getting the same calls," I quickly responded. "In fact, a delegation came into my office to confront me on the same issues. The church council has called a special meeting tonight. That is why I am happy we are having this exchange this morning, " I said.

Again, we paused, both reflecting on where the conversation might take us.

"I cant' find anything to accuse you of, anything to reprimand you for. After all, you didn't go down the Ave. inviting them to come up and camp on the porch. You came to work and there they were. Right?"

"Right. They set up their den all on their own. But they aren't a pack of wolves. Whoever said the twelve disciples were clean-shaven, showered, neat, and respectable? Smelly fisherman with dirty feet, that's who they were, and they slept wherever they could put their heads down. They drank wine, who knows how much."

He downright chuckled. "I think the religion editor is right: there's a story here. The Pharisses, the Sadduces, and the Roman Empire have all got your number. But as I see you and listen to you, I believe you will stay faithful to the Jesus who already called you. He didn't tell you where the path went. The call was "Follow me." I got the same call.

For now, it has taken me to the Bishop's chair. But this is only temporary. You and I are both on the way. Consider me alongside. Bless you."

Short and sweet. What more was there to say? We had connected. With that, I left his office, sent onward with deep gratitude and affirmation. I would return to his words and trust in his accompaniment as the story unfolded. Little did I know what was to come next.

Chapter Two

WHO IS OUR NEIGHBOR?

round six-thirty, the rains came. An eerie darkness, whistling winds, and a chill penetrated the marrow of the bones. It was such a frightful night, even for Seattle, I wondered if anyone would come. But, one by one, they came dripping in from the parking lot at the back of the building, accustomed to the downpours of the great Northwest.

Some joked about it, but others obviously wanted to get to work and get home again, their spirits dampened and irritable. I could not help but wonder how the men sleeping outside were coping with the tempest. Characterized as lazy, they struggled hard to survive on the streets. While we sat in a warm, lighted conference room drinking hot coffee, they huddled not far away, shivering and fevered under wet blankets.

Eileen Wagner, council chair, invited Sally Rogers to lead us in opening devotions. Whether by coincidence or divine plan, the text was on the Good Samaritan. The key question, "Who is our neighbor?"

I raised it again at the start of my pastor's report. "Who is our neighbor?" I waited, curious to hear answers. Their first response was, "Those who live around the church," the assumption being, other white middle-class property owners who have invested time and money in preserving the block.

"But what about the men on the porch? Are they our neighbors?" I asked. Then I told them about the morning meeting with the three from the neighborhood.

Clarence Pankowsky did not hesitate to express his position. "You're talking apples and oranges here. Let's not confuse one topic by introducing another. The congregation has responsibility to keep this block respectable. We don't live here. We don't have to put up with their antics all through the night. Quite honestly, I wouldn't want them across the street from my house. Who could sleep with those drunks howling under the window?"

"Wait a minute," Sally Rogers said. "The neighbors who complained do not live across the street. They live at the end of the block and across the alley. Their main interest is in protecting the value of their property. Is that our main concern?"

So the discussion began to take shape. We discovered that defining "neighbor" in a Biblical sense takes one into a deep probe for meaning, not only of the term but of self and relationship. That evening stretched out into weeks of soul searching and discovery.

Meanwhile, the delegation of three from the neighborhood began a concerted effort to force the men off. They contacted realtors, public health officials, the Chamber of Commerce, and the Bishop's office, requesting that pressure be applied for immediate action.

The church council determined that rather than heighten the conflict, the men should be asked to leave. I was directed to deliver the message. I anguished over the request, but realizing that it wasn't my property and they were the elected representatives of the congregation, I reluctantly agreed. I told myself that the news had best come from me.

Chapter Three

MIDNIGHT ON THE PORCH

It was midnight. I came to the porch alone. Eight red brick steps, centered by an iron handrail, led from the sidewalk up to the porch and were dimly visible under the borrowed light from the street. Beyond the arched overhang, I caught the outline of six men camping on blankets and sleeping bags. They went by their street names: "Patch John," "Spider," "Teardrop," "Loose," "Patrick," and "Wolfman."

"Evenin', Pastor June," Teardrop greeted me. They called him that because he had a small birthmark just under his right eye, shaped like a tear.

They were seated in a half circle, quietly talking. Nobody rose, but they smiled and nodded cordially as I came up the steps. I never felt afraid with them. We had established a respect among us, and we connected in the Spirit.

"Not a bad night, eh?" I responded. "Everybody doin' okay?"

"I got a letter from my ma today. She wants me to come back for her birthday the end of the month, but there's no way. I ain't got no money to do that. She's all the way down to L.A.," Teardrop said.

"How old is she gonna be?" Wolfman asked, in a low guttural voice that growled from the back of his throat.

"Seventy somethin'. I don't know. I lost track. If I did go, she'd just want me to stay there. She'd cry and carry on and beg me to settle down, get a wife, and give her some grandkids. She just don't get it. California ain't my scene no more." Everybody seemed to understand that statement.

Spider grinned. Feathery wisps of thin, purple hair twisted in the wind on top of his narrow peaked head, like a web. His squeaky voice was such a contrast to Wolfman's deep, throaty groans that it surprised me when he began talking.

"I was thinkin' of my ma today. I seen a scraggly stray dog runnin' loose in the alley. Took my mind to Lulu, a doggie I found on the playground when I was in the third grade. Lulu was a beauty. White and black and fluffy like a bunny. But somebody had crushed her spine. Her rear quarters didn't work so good. Like when she made a run for the school steps, she'd tumble backwards halfway up to the top. Sweet. That's what Lulu was. Just a dear. She kept comin' round and took a real shine to me. Nobody claimed her so I took her home."

"Oh boy. I can see it comin'. Your ma had a fit when you drug in a crippled stray," Teardrop said.

"That wasn't the worst. Not only did her legs give out, she dropped poop all over the house."

"So poor Lulu went back on the streets, right?" asked Patch John.

"You'da thought so. But my ma just picked up the poop with a Kleenex like them pellets was gifts of love. There wasn't a meanness in either of them, Ma or Lulu. Ma would take that dog in her lap and talk to her for hours, sayin' 'Somebody beat you up, Baby, and damaged your controls. I don't like your poopin' around, but I know you ain't doin' it on purpose. No dogcatcher is goin' to put you to sleep."

Spider thought a minute and then added, "I guess my ma feels that way about me, too."

"What kinda dog was Lulu?" Wolfman growled from the darkened corner of the porch.

"Sounds like a SHIT-TOO to me," Teardrop laughed.

We all laughed and then things got quiet.

Patch John shifted to a sitting position, his one eye shining in anticipation. It was as if he knew something was coming. That was my cue to begin. It was chilly, and I needed to be on my way home.

"Guys, I came to tell you something. You may stay the night, but then the church council says you have to leave. I'm sorry. This is not working out."

Loose, the poet who played the guitar, broke the stunned silence with bitter sarcasm. "I thought you was the pastor here. I thought this was the church. Now I know it's no different than any place else. The toilets in this building flush the same stuff down that every other toilet in the city flushes! This place is empty most hours of the week. We bring soul to it. We stand guard at the gate all through the dark times in the night. The rest of you are asleep. Throw us out and you'll see. The building will be an abandoned shell."

That stung. He knew it would. I left, saying no more. It was a long, restless night for me, with little sleep. I determined that I had to share the story.

In the pulpit, the following Sunday, I told the congregation about my late-night visit to the porch.

"I was directed by the church council to tell the men on the church steps that they must leave. They have done nothing but look to us for friendship and shelter. Sending them away is counter to the spirit of Jesus. These men are our brothers. Sending them away is an evasion of our responsibility. Moving them inside is hiding them behind our walls so the community can feel more comfortable.

"As it is now, they are showcased on the corner. Out there. And it becomes increasingly difficult to just walk past or step over them. Day after day, we of the community taste them in our mouths, smell them in our nostrils, hear them in our ears. They are flesh and blood, the Word incarnate drawn near to us. Do we have the courage to discover for what purpose they have come, or would you have us wash our hands of them?"

That stirred the fires.

Chapter Four

THE BRIDGE

ileen Wagner, feeling her power as the chair of the church council, took it upon herself, without anyone's knowledge or approval, to orchestrate a meeting. Notices were posted throughout the area and sent to members of the congregation and neighbors, announcing a public gathering in the sanctuary the following Sunday at 3:00 p.m., to discuss the situation with the men sleeping on our porch.

The notices were on church stationery, using church postage and secretarial time. True, Eileen was following her own conscience and taking responsibility as council chair, but it was not a team play. I felt betrayed and angry, and told her so. It was too late. The invitations were out, and conversations and speculations were running throughout the community.

Mahatma Gandhi once said, "To make any progress, we must not make speeches and organize mass meetings, but be prepared for mountains of suffering." I started to prepare.

On the following Sunday afternoon, a crowd gathered in the sanctuary. I sat at the back, determined not to say anything. It was the congregation's work, I told myself. It was not about me. It was about them and their dealing with the porch scene and the neighbors. I would just listen.

Then, a newspaper clipping, showing a black man with a knife attacking a white man on the steps of the Boston courthouse, was passed along the pew. It had nothing to do with the situation. The racial implications and the hint of violence conjured up fears that were unfounded.

Grace Updown, a 23-year-old black graduate student who had recently joined the new members' class came to the back and said, "Pastor June, you started this. You must speak."

I could not ignore her.

I rose and walked down the center aisle to the front, feeling my repressed anger surfacing in the back of my neck. Eileen, who was chairing the meeting, reluctantly gave me the floor. I took a deep breath, surveyed the crowd, and began.

"Since I am your pastor, I think I have a responsibility to express my feelings. I didn't plan to say anything. I was disciplining myself to listen and keep silent. But this newspaper clipping has been circulating throughout the pews. I don't know who started it on its way, but it is not acceptable. I appeal to you to take the high road. Racism, the threat of violence, and the rejection of the homeless are not in keeping with the mission of this congregation. Jesus made that abundantly clear. Let us reason together, pray together, and listen to the conscience of the spirit within us."

I paused, my heart racing, and then confessed, "It is taking all that I have to control my anger. Forgive me, but I look to you for more than a knee-jerk reaction to this kind of emotional blackmail."

Lifting the newspaper article high for all to see, I quietly withdrew to my seat in the back.

Immediately, Jim Haney, an older member who had shown considerable interest in the homeless, rose to support me.

"Our pastor is right. That news article has no bearing on our situation," he said. "I don't know who brought it, but for me it only damaged their case."

Emily, the neighbor woman who had come to my office, stood up and told us about walking her small dog Petunia in the early hours of the morning past our steps. She said the men sleeping on our porch had obviously been drinking and one shouted slurred comments at her that were offensive. Tension mounted as the discussion began to turn to confrontation.

I wondered if Eileen anticipated this when she set up the meeting. Not only neighbors, but members of the church spoke out against continuing "this nonsense" with the "derelicts" on the steps, "desecrating our beautiful church."

At the peak of exchange, Clarence Pankowsky, a single member who ordinarily withdrew from controversy, moved that a task force representing neighbors, community organizations, and members of the congregation be appointed to study alternatives and report back with recommendations to the church council within a month. The motion was seconded and passed.

I slipped out the front entrance, going straight to my car in the parking lot. Driving down the hill, I was blinded by the late afternoon sun. Suddenly I felt an overwhelming loneliness.

Loose's words would not leave me. "I thought you was the pastor here. I thought this was the church. It's no different than any place else."

"But it IS different, damn it!" I shouted as I swung onto the University Bridge toward home. Yet, when I pressed the "How?", no clear answer came.

The orange sky spread its cloudy pinions wide over the ship canal, burning strong against the encroachment of early night. Sometimes the classic old bridge opens her jaws to allow ships to move through *en route* to Lake Union. More than once, I have been delayed waiting for their passage. It was unpredictable, another sign of how things change within the span of a short time. I had to trust the flow, be patient, and wait as lines of cars stopped, giving way to the ships. No matter how urgent I thought it was for me to get on with it, I could not move until the huge steel jaws of the drawbridge closed, the traffic geared up for the green light, and I could join the caravan across the silver bridge that delivered us over the waters to the other side.

I had no control. A helpful metaphor indeed. Fortunately, no large vessels were in sight that night, only small crafts capable of gliding underneath without intervention.

My tiny mother-in-law apartment was dark and empty as I entered. The only light was the red blinking light on the answering machine. Already people were registering their opinions.

As usual, I had neglected to stop at the market on the way home. All I had in the house was a slice of bread, a banana, and herbal tea. I wasn't that hungry, anyway. I missed my children. I missed cooking large meals that helped them to grow and get strong. I set five place settings around the table every day for years. Now I sat alone in restaurants eating too much, or I came home tired and ate too little.

By ten o'clock, I was too sleepy for my customary Sunday night bubble bath. Exhausted, I climbed between the soft sheets and within minutes was drifting away, but not before I heard Emily whisper, "Wonderful! So it is all taken care of, then."

"Not quite, Emily. Not quite," I mumbled, "Not quite...not..." and I was gone.

* * * * *

Eileen wasted no time. The next day, she appointed six people to serve on the task force. Attorney Coombs and Professor Rice from "the committee," were appointed to speak for the neighbors. That was no surprise. Monica Crystal of the Chamber of Commerce, and Slade Grant, a realtor, agreed to serve on behalf of the larger community. Jim Haney and Clarence Pankowsky filled the two congregational slots. That made six.

Before the allotted month expired, they held three short sessions, and came back to the church council with three proposals:

(1) That the church doors be posted with CRIMINAL TRESPASS signs;

(2) That violation of these signs would give the police authorization to come on the property and remove trespassers;

(3) That members of the congregation should canvass the area and ask for donations to pay the Yellow Cab Company to take the men to shelters in the city.

For me, it was unthinkable to post the church doors with CRIMINAL TRESPASS signs. Nor was it reasonable to treat the men like they were outlaws. The church was private property. Their "crime" was to be homeless and sick. Why should the police be allowed to arrest them for being on the church steps? Further, the shelters in Seattle were full. Where was the Yellow Cab driver supposed to dump them?

Eileen notified the council members that the report was ready for their review. In the weeks since the public meeting, an amazing thing had happened. Defenses lowered. Members of the congregation were having heart conversations, contacting council members, and requesting that an action plan be developed that would move us beyond name-calling, empty rhetoric, and fear tactics.

Jim Haney was an architect. While he was trained to design buildings, he also had a skill in seeing how people needed support and secure foundations. He took time to talk to people and hear their issues. As the council convened, he quoted Marshall McLuhan, "You know the message is getting through when the image begins to change." He went on, "If we have a message to give, then we have to change our image and the image of the men on our porch. To do that, we have to know them as real individuals and not stereotypes."

The social ministry committee decided to form a porch patrol made of volunteers from the congregation. Their purpose was to oversee the property, visit the men on the porch, and enforce expectations for behavior. Teams of two went each night, made entries in the log, and reminded whoever was on the porch that they were expected to be quiet, leave the place clean, and not drink while on the premises. But something far more profound began to take place through this ritual.

Gradually, the men on the porch came to know the teams and relate their stories to them. The patrol began to see human beings who smelled because they had no place to take a shower; who drank because they were afflicted with alcoholism; who urinated and defecated in the bushes because they had no place to relieve themselves. These were men who told war stories, used street names, mourned their dead, and cared for each other like brothers.

Observing them nightly, the porch patrol began to appreciate that it took a fierce courage to survive on the streets. There were as many reasons for being there as there were men. No one had the exact same story.

MISSION STATEMENT
FOR THE PORCH PATROL
AT UNIVERSITY LUTHERAN:

It shall be our mission to provide sanctuary, support, information, advocacy, and spiritual encouragement for the homeless who come to our doors.

Our Goals:

- To examine our own stereotypes and assumptions about street people.

- To exercise self-restraint, the capacity to listen without judgment, and to deepen commitment to Christ's Gospel in a changing, urban context.

- To provide a safe place for dialogue, referral, medical attention, and recovery of self respect.

- To be faithful ambassadors of hospitality and reconciliation instead of hostility and alien-ation, being peacemakers.

- To do our homework so we feel prepared to meet the call: Regular Bible study, review of issues, sharing solidarity and prayer-exposure to the city and others working with the same challenges

- To advocate for detox facilities, job training, low cost housing, and community responsibility.

- To build relationship and interpersonal communication with our visitors; maintain a Log for continuity as a help in establishing interpretation of our mission.

- To transform rather than conform and to trust the Spirit's wisdom and energies at work in us.

Chapter Five

CITY CENTER

There they were. Three of them. Sassy as molasses stuck on the sidewalk outside the Safeway store. I had my car window rolled down and picked up Wolfman's deep-throated chuckle as I passed by. A woman passerby was handing Patch John money and, as always, I prayed they would go inside the deli and get soup. I almost stopped, but I was running late.

In addition to the porch patrol, the council approved an all-night marathon set from seven in the evening to seven in the morning. Neighbors, homeless, city professionals, and members of the congregation were invited to go through the night together, visiting city streets and facilities for the homeless, returning to thrash out fears, impressions, and solutions to the crisis surrounding the men on the porch.

A melancholy rendition of *Bess, You Is My Woman* wailed from the boom box in the kitchen as I followed the sound through the darkened church lounge. Grace Updown was standing at the sink filling the forty-cup coffee maker.

"Hi, Pastor June. I'm filling the big pot for a long night. I even baked two dozen brownies," Grace said as I appeared at the kitchen door.

"I don't know how you do it. Full load in grad school, part time at the Women's Crisis Center, volunteer at the Teen Shelter every Friday night, PLUS a shift on the porch patrol. You're going to burn out here, kid!" I warned.

"Well now, let's just look at who's talkin', shall we?" Grace laughed. "I also brought us a stack of tapes to revive us at 3:00 a.m. Second wind time, know what I mean? I've never done an all-nighter like this. Not sure who or what to expect," Grace continued as she cut the brownies and arranged them on a plate.

"I know for sure that Sylvia Ross will be here. Remember her? The black woman police officer, single mother with the small daughter?" I asked.

"Sure. I met her one night on the porch. I don't see many other black faces around this place. She startled me when she came by late with some extra blankets for the guys. She told me she grew up near the Kingdome, the baseball stadium they're going to blow up. She's great. Who else?"

I had to think for a minute. "Let's see. The chaplain from Luther House in Pioneer Square, Tom Petrie. He's supposed to be retired, but he's on the job every night."

"You know, I've been in Seattle for almost a year and I still haven't been down to that section. It's not far from the ferry terminal, is it?" Grace asked as she switched to Wes Montgomery's rendition of *What the World Needs Now is Love, Sweet Love*.

"Good you are going tonight. Things change fast in this city. Developers and city planners don't want missions there, because they attract homeless and hurt tourism and business. Benches, where homeless slept in the square, are gone. Now, they hide in empty doorways or sleep under bridges and docks." I swiped a brownie.

"Tony Carlson, director of Nightwatch, promised to show, but he wasn't sure if he could get here right at seven. They depend on volunteers, and sometimes there aren't enough to meet the demands. Have you seen the long lines of homeless waiting to get a bed for the night?" I continued.

"I don't go into the center of downtown much. I know where Nightwatch is, but I've never worked there," Grace answered.

The lights in the lounge came on. Jack Brigstone appeared, his arms loaded with cartons of soda. I never felt in tune with Jack, although we were not adversaries. He had a smack of the fraternity brother in him. He volunteered for Evangelism because of his outgoing personality and talked a good game, but never rang doorbells. He whistled a lot. Jim Haney walked in right behind him, carrying bags of groceries, calm and steady as usual, ready for whatever was to come.

"Food! Strength for the night!" I said as I walked out of the kitchen to greet them.

Just then, Tony Carlson, true to his promise, walked in with a disheveled bearded man who scowled from beneath a baseball cap, its flaps down over his ears.

"The office is covered, so I got right up here. This is Sketch, one of my friends from Nightwatch. He's got a real story to tell, but sometimes he's a little shy, aren't you pal?" Tony informed everyone.

Injun Jim was also invited as one of the homeless, but he was too drunk to attend. He sat curled up out on the porch, gazing off into the happy hunting grounds. His input was needed, so someone went to lift him to his feet and carry him into the group. He passed out.

About halfway through the first part of the evening, the neighbors came. It was always the same three. I wondered what happened to all the others who showed up for the Sunday meeting. Jim offered them chairs, but they had no intention of going through the whole process with us. They came to restate their determination to rid the neighborhood of those men on the porch. The intensity of their frustration was evident. There was no middle ground. They wanted those men gone, now! There was nothing to learn or understand.

Sketch cringed at their insensitivity. He had suffered a lifetime of insult upon insult. Now he sat as a guest, having to absorb yet another attack. I finally interrupted. I explained that we had a tight agenda and they were stealing time. If they did not want to be open to learn, I told them they would have to leave.

They left, with their rude outburst vibrating through the group as we organized to go into the city. Breaking into teams, the marathon participants got into vehicles and left to go to assigned places downtown.

It was 3:00 a.m. when everyone returned to the church for refreshments. Stories, accusations, feelings of shock and anger, confessions of neglect and indifference, prayers, and tears all seeped through our weariness as we sat in a circle on the floor reflecting on the night's experiences.

I had gone with Grace Updown to the downtown precinct with the lady cop, Sylvia Ross. We rode in a squad car, listening to calls on her radio, searching the alleys and streets for possible trouble spots. Sylvia knew these streets: she had grown up in them. The central dispatcher reported domestic violence in the 2800 block of Emerson; a knife attack behind the municipal shelter on Windsor; medics' arrival on the scene of a three-car accident at the intersection of Broad and York; a drunk reported near Pike Place Market for indecent exposure; a call for help from a frantic woman who said her husband was beating their child—the monotonous voice on the radio droned an unrelenting chronicle of incidents throughout the city.

Sylvia was off duty, on special assignment for community education. Cruising downtown, picking up calls on the radio, and touring precinct headquarters gave us a slice of how it was night after night on the police force. We knew we weren't watching a television series. The script was being written as we lived at the center of the action. Real people were in peril, needing intervention and help.

I just kept looking out the car window, wondering where the daytime city had gone. I had been down here at night wearing my clerical collar, distributing sandwiches, listening to the lost, so it wasn't my first exposure to the nighttime scene. But looking at it with the police radio blaring in my ear unwrapped the horrors happening behind the doors and windows.

Someone told me once that walking at noon through the busy downtown crowds, past the boutiques and sidewalk cafes, you don't realize how many rats are watching from the corners or running in the sewers below. This image of rodents sent a quiver through me. I wished I was in my comfy bed, where I would ordinarily be this time of night, instead of fastened in a seatbelt driving through hell. I could see why anyone would prefer the steps at the church to this.

Now, assembled again at the church, we passed a plate of cookies and sat in silence for awhile, savoring the taste of chocolate chips while we tried to digest the images flashing in our minds.

Jim Haney, Mary Post, and Joyce James, all members of the porch patrol, visited a municipal shelter where rows of bodies were lined up side by side on the floor. Mary Post admitted her fears as she walked into an alley to wait at the door of the shelter for someone to come down to answer the bell. She imagined someone lurking in the shadows and was relieved when the bell was answered and a skeletal woman with eyes like an owl's directed her inside, where Joyce and Jim were waiting.

A freight elevator lifted them to the second floor of a sleazy dark warehouse. An attendant, barely visible in the shadows, stood behind a desk, as though checking zombies into a flophouse on a B movie set. The rods and cones in Mary's eyes needed time to adjust to the semi-darkness, she said.

Then, Joyce began her account of their visit. "The first person I saw was a white-haired woman wandering down the hall groaning about the bathroom. She collided with a skinny twist of a man, balancing a stem of ashes on his lips. The two grunted as they stumbled along in the darkened expansive space. Deep breathing, snores, gasps, and periodic cries escaped from inanimate lumps, laid shoulder to shoulder under thin blankets on the floor. The attendant told me that most were so exhausted being on the streets all day, they collapsed as soon as they arrived."

"But there were also the agitated souls, unable to trust sleep. They were tense, watching for someone to pounce on them from the floor of the deadened," Joyce said.

"I sure didn't blame the guys here at the church for refusing to stay there," Mary added.

No one spoke for a while. Then Beth Carsted, who had accompanied the chaplain to Pioneer Square, told of a wheelchair in a doorway. It looked abandoned, just parked there, covered with a mound of dirty blankets. She was walking by it when she realized someone was sitting in it. He stirred just enough to draw her attention. She stopped and moved closer. Though he never showed his face, sensing her movement, he began to make eerie sounds of distress.

"I whispered softly, so as not to alarm him. I told him not to be afraid, I meant no harm."

"He screeched, 'Get away from me!' "

"I still could not see him, but his unexpected shriek terrified me. I ran around the corner where Chaplain Petrie was standing. He said the man had no arms or legs. The chair in that doorway had been his home for months. A few trusted friends brought food and checked on him, and people hurried past, never realizing he was there." But now she knew, and she wept.

We all wept. Mary moved closer, put her arm around Beth, and just held her while she sobbed, "This is not right! There is a human being there. Tourists pass by, businessmen hustle to their offices, artists hang their gallery pieces, and we sip lattes in the sidewalk café right next to him. He is there, hidden in the doorway. Nobody sees him! What can we do?" Silence. Grief. Despair and guilt.

Finally, Jack Brigstone broke in, saying, "I have another kind of story."

He recounted his walk through Pike Place Market, alive in the daytime with fish peddlers, craftsmen, fresh fruit stalls, jesters, flowers, musicians, and milling streams of buyers and lookers. But after midnight it takes on a different atmosphere, when transients, drug dealers, prostitutes, and gangs frequent its many nooks and crannies.

That's why Jack was afraid when two husky, downtrodden men approached him on the sidewalk. His back stiffened, and he was about to turn and run when one said in a friendly voice, "Do you know if there's any place open for a cup of coffee?"

They had come from Texas on the tip that Seattle had lots of good jobs. That was three weeks ago, and they were running out of money and time. Engaged in a conversation with one of them, from the corner of his eye, Jack saw the other fellow pulling something out of his pants pocket. Was it a gun? A knife?

"I got my New Testament along. It's what's kept us going. Listen to what Paul says in Romans, 'If God be with us, who can be against us?'"

Jack accompanied them to an all-night coffee shop and then to the Nightwatch office, where the two got in line in hopes of getting a bed.

What at first threatened to be a long unending stretch of night, now swept along quickly as we plunged into the currents of emotions and stories. I watched faces around the circle as fatigue broke down the barriers and honest feelings began to surface. Their feet had touched the ground; they were connected to the walk. They blinked at the flashing neon lights, saw the grayness in the gutter absorb the fire of moonlight overhead, and waited for an inner light to illumine their path. Little by little through their sharing, a common truth defined itself: to run from or deny reality takes much more energy than to face it. Perhaps that is why the men have come to live on our porch, I said to myself.

Slumped on the floor like deflated balloons, the weary group mustered new wind. Outside, the sky was tinged with rose-colored dawn. I invited everyone to pick themselves up and gather in the sanctuary around the baptismal font.

An old spiritual poured from my lips, "*There is a balm in Gilead, to make the wounded whole, there is a balm in Gilead, to heal the sin-sick soul.*" As they walked behind me, they joined the singing. "*Sometimes I feel discouraged and think my work's in vain, but then the Holy Spirit revives my soul again.*"

Our voices echoed in the hollows of the empty sanctuary.

We formed a circle, holding hands with heads bowed. When we finished the song, we stood in silence. Morning filtered through the stained glass windows to the east, splashing our faces with multicolored lights. Our numb toes and fingers were restored with warm energy. Our arms enfolded each other, giving support, as we whispered words of peace. The dreaded journey into darkness was over, and we were hungry for bread. It was time to go to breakfast. Would the night's impact penetrate, or would we slip back into the comfort zone?

We stopped to get Injun Jim, who had staggered back to the porch in the middle of the night. Blurry-eyed and wrenching, he calmly straightened his messy long, hair and agreed to come along. None of the other boys was around.

It was too early for heavy traffic. Only a few cars passed us as we all walked down the hill toward the restaurant. Injun Jim struggled to keep pace with the group. The sky unfolded from a deep rose to a pink and finally yellow spray of radiance that illuminated the Olympic Mountains to the west. The city was awakening and we all felt on top of it. All, that is, except Injun Jim.

He couldn't eat. His body needed a shot of booze. His system couldn't handle the food. It craved alcohol. His hands began to tremble. Mary Post, Tom Petrie, and Jim Haney sat in a booth with him. Feeling powerless, Mary told him what he had heard so many times before: "Your only hope is to get help. Do you want to live?"

And, like so many other times, he said, "Yes. I am too young to die." And then he ran for the bathroom to unload the small taste he had taken of scrambled eggs.

There we sat, in a public restaurant where Injun Jim would not have been served if he hadn't come in with us. We were one party. We broke bread together at the same table. The high at the baptismal font was more than symbolic. It was a turning point. Injun Jim was affirmed and was invited to live. Everyone sincerely wanted him to accept the invitation.

After that morning, he disappeared from the porch. No one knew what happened to him—or maybe they weren't telling. Then one day, months later, one of the boys reported that Injun Jim had returned to his people on the reservation and gone into treatment. He was in recovery and had gotten a job.

Solomon's Portico: that was where, in the book of Acts, the disciples gave the beggar power to stand and walk and jump. Others recognized him as the one who used to sit at the Beautiful Gate and beg, and were astonished and perplexed at what had happened to him. One day when Peter and John, disciples of Jesus, were going up to the temple to pray, this man asked them for alms. Peter said, "I have no silver or gold, but what I have I give you; in the name of Jesus Christ of Nazareth, stand up and walk." And he took him by the right hand and raised him up and immediately his feet and ankles were made strong. Jumping up, he stood and began to walk (Acts 3:1-10).

It was not money that helped Injun Jim to recover. Someone saw him through the eyes of Jesus. Shared the table. Broke the bread. Invited him to live. Injun Jim's was the first in a series of miracles. Illness is an expression of personality and human interaction. The dynamics of relationship are both at the root of disease and at the place of its forgiveness and healing.

Chapter Six

HERE I STAND

Fortunately, the church secretary had the right name: Hope. Kind but tough, she was not swept away by the stream of strange folks who moved in and out of the outer office. She got them first. Every day had its surprises, but one morning, even she was astonished. She appeared in my doorway saying, "I think you better come out here."

There stood Patch John without his pants on. He wore a long suit coat, which covered his bare bottom, and shoes but no socks.

"I couldn't help it, Pastor June. I just shit all over my underwear, my pants, my socks, my shoes. I just woke up loaded with shit."

I thought I had seen it all, that nothing could faze me, but I must admit Patch John was quite a spectacle, and it was all I could do to keep from laughing.

"So, where are your clothes?" I asked, containing myself.

He looked embarrassed and ashamed.

"I threw them in the trash barrel."

"Well, we'll just have to get you some new ones. Go in the men's room and wash your legs."

"I already did that," he said sheepishly.

"All right, then come with me."

The two of us walked out of the church and down the hill toward a thrift shop on the Ave. We walked as fast as we could and said little to each other. I expected someone to honk their horn, or maybe a police officer to come and arrest John for indecent exposure.

"Be sure your suit coat stays buttoned," I cautioned, wondering how I managed to get into these situations.

When we reached the corner, the light changed, so we stood staring at the DON'T WALK sign. I wanted to drain down into the gutter, but thought of the hero of the Protestant Reformation, Martin Luther, who said, "Here I stand. I cannot do otherwise!" Would Martin have stood by a half-naked man with a patch over his eye in broad daylight, while hundreds of gawking drivers passed by?

The Thrift Shop had a dressing room in the back. Patch John went swiftly to hide in it while I selected a pair of pants, underwear, clean socks, and a sweatshirt from the racks. I had to guess his size. At least he was clean again; dressed again.

The clerk took my credit card without a hassle. When we stepped out of the store, Loose approached us on the sidewalk.

"Do you think they'd have a pair of shoes in there that would fit me? My soles are leaking and my feet are wet and cold."

"Does it ever end?" I wondered as I led Loose back into the store to find a pair of waterproof boots.

Chapter Seven

LOOSE

Before Loose came to Seattle, he was more or less taking the geographical escape route, treking around the country, trying to find the missing element. He didn't know what that was or how he could find it. He was lost.

He was 45, but looked 60. He wore a filthy baseball cap that covered his balding crown. Bags hung below his hooded eyes. Those were eyes clouded by angry, bitter disappointment. Furrowed wrinkles on ruddy cheeks mapped roads walked in solitary wandering. His red nose betrayed his drinking habits and popped out like the schnozzle of a circus clown.

Loose was trying to be somebody, but couldn't gain the attention he felt he warranted. Occasionally, he would write a poem or talk about a song he composed. He had a guitar that he couldn't play because the strings were broken. I offered to have them repaired, but then, of course, the excuse would be gone and he would have to demonstrate that he really could play the thing.

Like all the boys, he sustained himself with rot-gut, cheap wine. Mama Sui, the Vietnamese proprietor, kept a running tab for all of them at her mini-mart. She "managed their money." They had their assistance checks from the government mailed to her place, and she subtracted their booze as the month drained on.

Two beasts took residence in Loose's body. One, an arrogant lion that defied taming, the other, a lamb with a poet's soul and a heart willing to be sacrificed.

This dual nature became more pronounced when Blond Harry showed up one night on the porch, halfway to death. Divorced, he had two children and was the son of a prominent businessman who was active in another Lutheran church in the city. The family had tried everything to salvage Harry's life, but he was so entangled in alcohol addiction, there seemed nothing could dissuade him.

Loose took a position at his side. Blond Harry had diabetes, a disease that does not mix well with cheap Mogen David wine. Red flashing lights swirled through my office windows from emergency vehicles in the alley at all hours of the day and night.

Blond Harry got to be suicidal. Liquor and drugs drove him deeper into the valley of despair. His wife left him, his two children never saw him, and his pious parents' prayers were lost on him. He receded farther and farther from contact, dipping up and down between peaks of insight to the foggy swamps of timeless murky hallucinations. He was admitted to different hospitals, sobered up, talked to, and sent back out to die. Loose did not leave him.

Cold nights, heavy rains, and his lowered immunity made it hazardous for Blond Harry to stay on the alley steps, so Loose and a few others put a kitty together to rent a room in the upper floor of a house just back of the church. About twenty transients lived there. It was reputed to be a drug depot, but nothing had been firmed up on that. The neighbors were probably in an uproar about that place, too, but all we heard about from them was our porch.

Harry had a sofa in the middle of the living room traffic. Loose slept on the floor next to him. At least twice, I saw Loose come tumbling down the outside wooden steps that led to the second floor, so inebriated he could feel no pain!

But the night of the final call, when the red lights pulled up and the medics disappeared up those steps, Loose fell apart. Blond Harry was determined to die. There was nothing that would interrupt the course of his deepest desires. Loose left. Within hours, Blond Harry got his wish. His weary heart gave out. The family finally got him back in the church. This time, in a coffin.

It wasn't long before Loose was back on our porch finding solace in his bottle. His dreary eyes began to look yellow, and his hands trembled uncontrollably. It was clear that it would take more than I could give. Only some radical turning of the soul would forestall a death like Blond Harry's. Ghosts of others who had lived on that porch and hovered near death were around him.

Loose knew the consequences of his continuing to drink, and yet he compulsively consumed large quantities of wine. The lion that roared within him wasn't giving the lamb lying nearby much sleep. Day by day, he refused help, and day by day his condition deteriorated. No one could reason with him. It was another time of reckoning. I could not rescue him, but I still held to the miracle of amazing grace.

Jack had been on the porch patrol since it started. He was a member of the church council and chaired the evangelism committee. Jack was the ascending star of a newly merged insurance conglomerate. He was promoted to oversee three regions and jetted from territory to territory most of the week. It was difficult to imagine him as the in-charge person. Not that he didn't have the intellect or organizational savvy to wield such power, but he didn't seem to particularly value it.

He had lived in Alaska before he became a family man. His face grew animated when he dipped into tales of the wild times he'd had with the untamed lumberjacks and fishermen in the Yukon.

He had an identical twin brother. The two of them hiked the Appalachian Trail one summer, and if he wasn't recalling his adventures in Alaska, he was taking everyone back with him to that summer on the trail.

Somewhere in his past, he developed a keen interest in Reinhold Niebuhr, writer and professor of Christian ethics at Union Theological Seminary, New York. Niebuhr's insights explored how individual morality could overcome the politics and brutality of collective force.

While other parents shielded their children from contact with the low life on the porch, Jack dressed his two small daughters in their best dresses to introduce them to Patch John, Loose, and Patrick.

One Sunday morning, Loose wandered into church, asking the ushers where he could find Jack. They directed him upstairs to the Sunday school class Jack taught for teenagers. Loose had written a poem for him and wanted to personally deliver it.

The Birdem of Freedom

I Stand in The Stairway

With my Back To The Dungeon

The Gateway To Freedom —

So Close To my Hands —

But Voices Behind me —

Still Bitterly down me —

Fore Seeking Salvation —

They don't understand —

So Help me To Shoulder —

This Burden of Freedom —

And Give me the Courage —

To Be what I Can —

Loose's poem for Jack.

Jack was honored and invited Loose to read it aloud. On the streets, there were dogs that growled, shots that exploded in the dark, and knives that knew they were designed to cut. But for this moment, Loose participated in a world that was safe, where grace prevailed. Loose and Jack bonded with the kids who thought it was "cool."

It was after ten the next night when Jack arrived on the porch patrol. It was one of those rare weeks when he didn't have to fly out until Tuesday. He lived in Issaquah, on the east side of Lake Washington, and took the floating bridge over to Seattle.

The night was nasty. The rain soaked through his coat and into his skin. Jack realized firsthand how good it was to duck under the roof of the porch, away from the lightning and heavy downpour. The boys were lined up under their sleeping bags watching the storm. Loose opened his arms to Jack to give him an embrace. When Jack bent down to return the affection, he felt the burning hot cheeks of a man wrapped in fever.

"Loose. You are sick. You shouldn't be here on a damp night like this."

"That's what we've been telling him," Champ said. "But we don't have any other place to take him."

"Are you good enough to get up?" Jack asked.

"I don't know. I'm so weak I can't think," Loose whispered.

"Champ. Patch John. See if you can help him. I'll get the car and come around to the curb. We'll find a motel somewhere where you guys can get some sleep and get warm, or we'll have you all sick before we know it."

I heard the whole story the next morning. Champ told me every detail. Loose was so sick he couldn't take a swig from the bottle and keep it down! They loaded him into Jack's car and headed for a strip of cheap places with kitchenettes on Highway 99. Every time a truck whizzed past they got a blinding splat! on the windshield that momentarily caused Jack to lose sight of the road. Loose broke into sobs. His body convulsed with chills, and he talked about devils.

The Birdie Bye Motel was a dump. The boys had pooled their money once before to rent a room there. Jack cringed when the clerk showed them the room. Low wattage in the bulbs, cracks of thunder outside, and Loose's trembling body contributed to a sense of spooky terror, but at least it was dry and warm. Jack paid for three nights with his credit card.

It was 2:00 a.m. when Jack drove to an all-night pharmacy to get some over-the-counter meds for Loose. When he returned, they joined hands around Loose, who was sprawled out on one of the beds. Jack asked the holy angels to keep watch through the night and protect his own from any dangers.

As soon as he left, they turned on the television. It was a toy they seldom got their hands on.

* * * * *

I was meeting Karen, a casual acquaintance, for lunch at the far end of the Ave. The sidewalks were crowded with university students and visitors. As I passed the India restaurant and caught a sniff of their aromatic spices, I realized I was hungry. Long-time residents lamented the loss of fashionable dress shops, jewelry stores, and gift shops that once had attracted tourists and locals with money to spend. In former days, there had been sophistication and class in the clientele who came to eat in some of Seattle's fanciest restaurants.

But things had changed. Internationals moved into the area and opened and closed fast food cafes and junky souvenir hole-in-the-wall places that lured college students and drifters into the area and discouraged investors from gentrifying it again. Older people who used to come there stayed away, afraid of the street people.

I liked the character of the place. Whenever I walked along the Ave, I got intoxicated by the sensuous smells floating from a variety of ethnic eateries. I always expected the unexpected. Life was dynamic and alive. I was reflecting on that when, above the sounds of the sidewalk commotion, I picked up the faint whine of a siren. It was coming closer. No one paid attention, as it was common for ambulances and rescue units to streak through the streets *en route* to University Hospital. But this vehicle, with its flashing red light, stopped in the next block.

My lunch date, Karen Blake, waved to me from the window of the restaurant, but I ignored her, fixing my gaze toward the flashing lights. Usually, the call was for a street person. Somehow, I knew this time it was for one of the porch guys.

Karen beckoned, questioning if I saw her. She had come from West Seattle and had an appointment at 1:15 at the university to talk about teaching a course in childhood behavior. She always had a place she had to be, an agenda to meet, and more important things to do than have lunch with a friend. I had known her back East and often wondered why I continued the relationship.

"Over here," Karen called as I came through the door. "I already ordered. Hope you don't mind."

I slipped quickly into the booth, preoccupied with the scene outside.

"What's going on out there?" Karen asked. Then, without waiting for an answer she added, "I ordered the clam chowder and half a sandwich. How are you?"

"I'm fine, I guess. Busy," I said absent-mindedly.

"You're not still messing with those street people, are you? Honestly, I don't know how anyone could give them the time of day. They are so filthy and lazy. One just asked me for money for a cup of coffee. I didn't give him anything, of course. I told him to get a job!" Karen said as she swallowed a pill. I noticed she had a full pillbox of Prozac in her purse. Like so many fast-paced urbanites, she depended on anti-depressants to lift her confidence and mood. Was that so different from the boys who depended on their booze to get them through the day?

She sat across from me like a solid chunk of butter waiting to be dissected into pads of appointments, assignments, and memos. I stared at her, wondering how long it would be before she melted down. A wave of sadness came over me as I recognized how separate our lives had become.

"Yes. Well, this matter of getting a job isn't always so easy, you know. Malnutrition, internal bleeding, liver complications, pneumonia, diabetes, flu, substance abuse—just to name a few maladies from living on the streets," I pointed out.

"Well, I didn't come to talk about that anyway!" Karen laughed. "I don't have much time. You were late."

What she really wanted to talk about was HERSELF getting a job. The entire conversation focused on the upcoming interview and her anxiety. The salary was a major topic. She didn't want to settle for less than she was worth just because she was a woman. Her monologue continued for fifteen minutes, until the clock struck one and she twittered her way into the ladies room for one last look in the mirror before saying goodbye.

I remembered when Betty Friedan was prophet most high in the feminist movement, and how I used to indulge in long hours of talk with women such as Karen. Those were important then, but somehow the movement had gone beyond and left Karen stuck in her anxiety. I felt relieved as we went our separate ways. I didn't bother to eat.

The ambulance was still in the next block, so I walked closer. The person who lay prostrate on the sidewalk was Loose. His beard was sticky with red blood that trickled down from a cut on his cheek. His Irish eyes weren't smiling anymore, but gazed vacantly from dark holes sunk on either side of his broken nose. The medics lifted him onto a stretcher, carried him into the van, and closed the doors. His vital signs had to be monitored to determine whether or not he needed to be taken on to the emergency room.

Near me, the police were questioning a man. I overheard him say, "He just staggered right out in front of my car. There was nothing I could do."

I stood with three or four curious onlookers, waiting for the next move. I knew the medic who jumped out from the back of the van and asked him where Loose would be taken.

"The trauma center at Harborview. Check there."

Loose was a great storyteller. My mind went back to the night he got off on one of his adventures. We were all on the porch when he took center stage.

No one believed Loose when he said Agatha Christie invited him for a drink at the Hotel Pera Palas in Istanbul. He said he met her on the Orient Express train where he worked in the kitchen. One night, she ordered dinner in her private compartment.

"Who the hell is Agatha Christie?" interrupted Patch John.

"She wrote mystery books," Lenny volunteered.

"That figures. She found herself a new character!"

"She found me, that's for sure. When I knocked, she asked me in, and when I put the tray down, she offered me a glass of sherry. So, I sang her a song. She musta liked it because when we got to Istanbul, I sang it again at the Pera Palas."

"So, that's where your drinkin' problem started, eh?" Teardrop quipped.

"In where was this place?" Wolfman growled.

"Turkey."

"You're the turkey," Patch John roared.

They all had a good laugh. That's how it went, night after night. That bunch of them—Loose, Patrick, Patch John, Lenny, Wolfman, Teardrop, Spider—whoever showed up. Nobody knew real names and nobody knew true stories from false.

As quickly as the ambulance appeared, it disappeared, its siren disrupting my reverie.

I walked up the hill to the church, wondering if Loose would make it this time. Why did I even care? The irascible fool. He refused help. If he didn't want to live, why should I pray that he would?

There were five messages on my desk when I returned to the office. There was much to attend to in the congregation. My plate was full without Loose.

Chapter Eight

PROS AND CONS

The janitor went at 6:30 that Sunday morning to find five full sleeping bags blocking the entrance door to the sanctuary. The first service wasn't until 8:30, but it took time to clear the porch and then disinfect it. An acrid order of ammonia seeped from the cement. Cigarette butts sprinkled the steps. Underneath the bodies, piles of cardboard insulated against the cold.

The boys were hard to rouse. Gradually, they opened their eyes and agreed to move. This was a church, after all, and on Sunday mornings, they knew the members used the front entrance.

Even with three pails of strong disinfectant, the lingering smell of urine couldn't be erased. There was muttering as people entered the sanctuary. Some had been members of this congregation for many years and felt deeply wounded that the "House of the Lord" should be desecrated. "Cleanliness is next to Godliness." "This is an outrage!" "Someone has to do something about this!"

The mumbling in the lounge finally prompted Karl Wheeling to make an appointment to come in to discuss the matter with me. He was a professional counselor, so I expected him to understand the problems of the homeless. I liked Karl, even though we had never connected on a social basis. Once we had talked about a movie, but we never actually put it on the calendar.

He owned his own condo and had a close circle of friends in the complex. I wondered why he had never married, since he was attractive and intelligent. Now that he was in his fifties, his hair was graying and fine wrinkles clustered around his eyes. He wore artsy, colorful, casual clothes, spoke softly, and drove an antique automobile upon which he lavished much attention. A strange combination of composure and poise on the surface, mixed with a strain of unpredictable kookiness simmering underneath.

I picked up my pastry and two tall lattes at Starbuck's on my way to our appointment at my office. I felt genuinely cordial, looking forward to talking to him about the situation on the porch. I assumed he had come to form an alliance. He had not. He arrived upset.

We exchanged a few stock greetings: "Good morning...let me take your coat...help yourself" before he made his position clear. His empathy was aligned with the property committee and the legacy of his dear father, who took tremendous pride in maintaining his congregation's building back East.

"Pastor, I am ashamed to invite people to attend worship because of the stench. Furthermore, one morning on my way to church, I met some of those men coming down the hill from here, and they looked unkempt and disgusting. I am confused and disturbed that any pastor would tolerate such abuse of a beautiful building like ours. My father took such pride in my family church back home," he said.

"I know. Same here. I watched them bring the stones to build the walls of my home church back in Minnesota. My dad would say every night after supper, 'Come with me, Junie. Let's go see what they did today.' And that building grew and grew right in front of my eyes. I carry a lot of sentimental attachment to that place," I responded. "But you and I know that the church is more than bricks and mortar. Human beings are living stones. The real church."

Karl flared, "Don't preach at me!"

Now that was a bee sting. His voice spoke for many, and he knew I knew it. A large part of the yearly budget was allocated to keeping the place in shape. Many volunteered hours to polish the pews, press the altar cloths, shine the silver, and repair the roof. Landscaping, trimming, and planting went on year-round in the yard. It hurt to remove the bushes out front when the health department pointed out that the boys were using them for cover when they defecated in the night.

"Karl, let's not do this. I need you to be with me. Can we keep communicating about this?" I offered.

"I doubt that I will find the time. My office schedule is very demanding. I just hope you have heard me clearly," he said, looking at his watch. "I must go now."

I felt a tightening in my stomach as Karl walked out of my life.

"Hope," I called to my secretary. "There's an extra latte here that hasn't been touched. You want it?"

After his passionate visit, Karl left the congregation. I called him, but the calls were not returned. I left my card on his condo door, but he never appeared in church. Nor did he officially transfer his membership. He just took time out to attend another congregation in the district, probably hoping I would be forced to leave and things would return to their normal state.

He was the exception, because most members came through the back door, off the parking lot. They never crossed paths with the boys. If they did, they were more kindly, recognizing that the congregation was, in fact, running a hospice unit for benign drunks searching for hope.

Chapter Nine

FOR EVERYTHING
THERE IS A SEASON

Because winter in Seattle is generally mild compared to the blizzards I left behind in the Midwest, I was surprised one morning to wake up to snow. When I stepped outside, I left footprints on the walk. The wind forced me back into the warmth of the kitchen and hot coffee.

Fortunately, it was New Year's Day, so people would not have to get to work. The whole city was paralyzed when even a trace of snow dusted the pavement. Seattle is set upon seven hills, and when the streets get glazed with ice, cars go out of control in the hands of inexperienced drivers.

I viewed it as divine intervention. The snow gave permission to curl up with a book by the fireplace. Relaxed and cozy, I took time to prepare breakfast and turned on a tape of choral music. What a luxury, just to be home for the day without pressing demands.

And then they occurred to me. The boys! The boys on the freezing porch! There would be no one around the church this morning to check if they were all right. The usual internal dialogue began.

"You're the pastor. You have defended their being there. It got down to freezing last night. What if they need help?"

"Give me a break. Trust that someone will go by there and..." Even as the internal argument continued, I brushed my teeth, dressed, stepped into the cold day, and drove to the church. Much as the firefighter hears the alarm bell, I was activated by the silent alarm of the boys in the cold.

Three of them were there. Buried under sleeping bags and blankets, they huddled together for body warmth.

"Happy New Year, boys!" I shouted. "Why? WHY didn't you report to a shelter when you knew the weather report said snow and frigid temperatures?" Nobody stirred. "Are you frozen under there?" I kicked the bundle to test for life.

Groans, barely audible mumbles, steamed out from under the heap. Boldly, I pulled back the covers.

"So, who do we have here this morning?" I snapped.

Loose's Kris Kringle nose, red as a Christmas bulb, popped before my eyes.

"Loose! I thought you moved to the blowhole back of the Safeway. Isn't warm air coming up there?"

Patch John answered, exposing his black face against the white day, "We wouldn't let him stay there. Too close to the alley. We were afraid some truck or car would swing in and slide on the ice and hit him."

"Look. It was New Year's Eve. You could have just ridden a free bus all night and stayed warm," I said.

"We got our love to keep us warm," Loose grinned, pulling a bottle of the forbidden fruit from under the sleeping bag to his lips.

"I get really sick of you guys, you know that?"

"We're sorry, Pastor June. But we don't like those shelter places. Everybody's coughing and sick. They line you up shoulder to shoulder on the floor and turn out the lights. The air is bad. People smell. And one night, a crazy guy pulled a knife on somebody lying next to him. It's not safe," Patch John explained.

"You get this locked-up feeling. Some bully, only two days off the street himself, orders you around. The mission gives him a prayer and a white tee shirt, and all of a sudden, he's in charge of your life!" Loose snarled.

"Look. You have to start thinking of a plan. This porch can't be your place indefinitely." I wondered how many times I had made that profound statement, not only to the boys, but to City Hall, the merchants on the Ave, the ecumenical partnership, the members of the congregation, and the neighbors who kept their campaign alive to get rid of me. As though getting rid of me would solve the crisis.

Loose sat up straight. "The mayor, the police chief, the city attorney, they don't have it right. They're making the wrong decisions. The other night, a jar head, bigger than his car, pulled up to the curb and grabbed my sack. He took my two bottles, opened them up, and poured them out on the sidewalk. I panhandled two days for that medicine. And he just dumped it in the street. He was a policeman doing what the taxpayers were payin' him to do, but that don't fix nothin'. It just makes a person empty and sad.

"Pastor June, I pray every night that I won't wake up. If it weren't for you and the other folks who come, I'd say life's got no invitation for me. Why can't the holy angels come and just get me out of this?"

Ignoring him, I asked, "Who's this third guy?" as I uncovered his face.

"That's Lenny. Don't you know him?" Patch John asked.

"Can't say that I do. Judging by the blood trickling out of his mouth, I may never get the opportunity. I'm going in to call 911. Just stay here until the medics come."

Lenny was taken to Harborview Hospital and admitted to intensive care. I went to see him when his life was in the balance. All I could do was pray silently by his bed and report back to the boys that he was still alive. Gradually, when he regained consciousness, he was moved to the rehab unit, still very sick but over the crisis. When I returned to see him there, he recognized me.

"Welcome to the new year. You've been a pretty sick man. I'm Pastor June. I bring you greetings from Loose and Patch John. They want to know how you are. What should I tell them?"

Lenny opened his eyes wider, gazing intently at this woman who stood by his hospital bed. As he was staring at me, I got a straight look at him. His features were refined, and even though his eyes were weary, they had intelligence. Strange to say about such a weathered face, but it was aristocratic and handsome in spite of everything. When he spoke, his speech was slurred.

"I'm alive. I guess that's the big news," he said gently, never taking his attention away from my face. "They say I lost a lot of blood. It'll take a while to get my strength back."

"Do you have any family?" I asked.

"Not close by. I come from the eastern part of Washington. My wife is dead and my kids are all grown. I've kinda lost touch with them. It's best that way, I think. We're all on our own now." He sounded sad.

"Don't you think they would want to know you are here?" I continued.

His expression suddenly became apprehensive. "No. I don't want anybody getting them stirred up about me. Just leave things as they are, okay? I don't want anybody calling them. I mean it. Leave it alone."

He began coughing. The color drained from his cheeks. A nurse came in and indicated I should leave, as Lenny still wasn't too stable.

When I returned the next day, he was sitting in his chair. He looked more alert, and smiled when he saw me at the door.

"Sorry if I upset you yesterday. Forgive me, but you don't seem like the kind of man who would be living on the street. Share something about yourself so I feel like I know you better."

He hesitated. His hazel eyes searched my face again, as though measuring just what was safe to disclose.

"I've had a lot of good in my life. I had good parents. A beautiful wife. When she died, I fell apart. Started drinking. It took me down. I'm not proud of it, but here I am," he reached for a glass of water, his hand shaking.

His thick black hair was beginning to show silver around the temples. I guessed he was in his late fifties. A few wrinkles on his forehead betrayed the stress of his lifestyle, and the blood loss had obviously taken its toll. He was very weak. Yet, even in his weakness, he was proud. He was not sharing the whole story. But why should he?

We tell what we feel safe to tell. Nothing escapes our lips if the guard of our conscience forbids the words to be spoken. Some things are not meant to be shared. Even in a hospital unit for critical care, Lenny wasn't opening the gate to his guts. I respected that and left him alone. Someday, perhaps, he would trust me, but he wasn't there yet.

When Lenny died a few weeks later, the hospital called and said he had listed me as his next of kin. They wanted to know if I was aware of any family that should be notified. I didn't even know his proper name. Like all of the boys, he went by a street name. He had mentioned brothers in the carpet business in eastern Washington. In a casual conversation one night while he was in the hospital, he alluded to his children. The boys said he talked all the time about his wife who had died of cancer. But for some mysterious reason, he didn't want the family to know where he was, and answered simply to the name of Lenny.

The social worker who was calling said there were a few personal things, his clothes, a cosmetic kit, a bloody handkerchief, and an empty wallet. She asked permission to dispose of them.

But then she added, "There is an envelope that is addressed to you. He's been in and out of here over the last six weeks. He would have lucid moments and would sit up in his bed getting his thoughts down on paper. Once I asked him to read it, and he put it under his pillow. I think it was a letter to you. It must be what is in the envelope. Do you want to pick that up, or should we mail it to you?"

"Send it to me here at the church," I told her, knowing that my schedule for the weekend allowed no time to get it. Then,

I agreed to call them if I got further information.

He was being taken to the morgue, and they would be running a check on him through the Veterans' Administration. Fingerprints and things.

"What was the cause of death?" I asked.

"Internal bleeding. Transfusions weren't enough to save him. He died soon after he was admitted early this morning."

"Where did they find him?" I continued.

"In a doorway of an empty store on University Avenue. That's what the medics told me in the Emergency Room."

"That was his office. He had a chair and table there, and made appointments with people to meet him," I recalled.

"What people?" she asked.

"People like me, I guess. And his cronies. Once in a while he'd give a haircut. He was a good barber."

"I have to hang up now. Things are busy here. I'll send you the letter," the woman from the hospital said.

I thought about Lenny. I thought about the staff at the hospital and what they saw and did. Most of all, I wondered why he listed ME as his next of kin!

Chapter Ten

THE LETTER

I closed the door, sat down at my desk, and opened Lenny's letter. The envelope was wrinkled, as though he had been carrying it for some time. Inside, the letter started in ink and was written in clear penmanship. But later, it was more difficult to read, and was finished in pencil with a gray lead. He must have struggled near the end, because lines were scratched out, edited and re-written. Watermarks smeared the last paragraph and I wondered if the blurs were from his tears.

> *Dear Pastor June,*
> *This letter will be in your hands after I*
> *am dead. I am writing to you because*
> *I feel I want to confess the secrets*
> *that I have carried these last five*
> *years on the street. I used to go to the*
> *Catholic Church and was told that the*

priest would keep everything confidential. You have been my priest, so I am trusting you with my story, hoping you will continue praying for my soul and asking God to forgive me of my grievous sins.

My name is not Lenny. I was baptized Franklin Lloyd Wilkerson. My parents were well-to-do farmers who provided richly for me and loved me dearly. I had two brothers and a sister. We were a close family.

I went to college and on to graduate school, earning a Ph.D. in Education from the University of Chicago. More than anything, I wanted to come back to where I grew up and teach in the small, remote high school near our family farm. It was a rural school in eastern Washington that drew pupils from all over the surrounding valley. (We were about two hours outside of Spokane.) There was a vacancy for a math teacher and I applied. I never liked Chicago. It was too big and dirty. I missed the smells of the *country. It may sound trite, but I felt I wanted to give something back to the people that had supported and encouraged me when I was an adolescent.*

The first day I came into my classroom, Sarah Jane stood at the door with fresh-baked brownies. She taught home economics and wanted to welcome me to the faculty. I must admit, I wanted to taste her, not the brownies she held in her hands. She was a vision standing in the threshold. From that moment on I loved her with all my heart. And the more I discovered, the more I loved her.

On weekends we went to the mountains to hike and ski. Her slim body twisted and turned down the slopes with the precision of a professional. In summer, we kayaked and went for picnics. After school, I would go down the hall to her test kitchen and sample goodies her classes had concocted. We both loved music and never missed the music department's choral concerts or band programs.

Our wedding was a glorious event. We were married at the farm, two years after we met. My parents decided to retire from the farm and move to a new house in Spokane. They asked if we would like to have the farmhouse. My brother agreed to farm the land. He owned the adjacent property and lived three miles down the road with his wife and two kids.

Sarah Jane kept teaching the first year, but when she got pregnant, decided to stay home. Those were the days when women did that. I was very happy.

Then the principal resigned and I was asked to take his position. It meant more money, but more respon-sibility, too. We talked it over and Sarah Jane urged me to accept the offer. I did. And it turned out to be a wise decision. I was able to introduce lots of ideas and attract young, creative teachers. Our school district was growing and we were experienc-ing challenges we had not faced before.

Our first child was a son. Over the next twelve years, we parented five more offspring. In all, there were four girls and two boys. Each of them was distinct. Sarah Jane raised them, I must admit. I was so taken up with my administrative tasks at school; I wasn't around as much as I should have been. I tell you all of this so that you know how much I respected and adored that woman.

We were married forty years. When the children left to pursue their own dreams, we traveled to Europe, Mexico, and Alaska. I didn't drink much in those days, but when we went to dinner or late night dancing, I got to ordering drinks. Then, I started stocking a liquor cabinet in the dining room. It got so that I could hardly wait to leave school and get home for my cocktails. I avoided evening meetings whenever I could because I was becoming a closet drinker.

Sarah Jane loved me too much to argue about it. She refused to drink with me, and sometimes she would disappear early after dinner with a good book, leaving me alone with my bottle. I denied that I had a problem. I just enjoyed a relaxing drink or two at the end of a hard day. Now that all the children were gone, the place was too quiet. I told myself that I needed consolation.

Then came Sarah Jane's announcement. She had been to the doctor's office and in a routine physical; they had found a large lump in her breast. The doctor scheduled a biopsy. She hadn't told me about it because she thought it would be disturbing. Without my knowing, she went to the out-patient day surgery for the procedure. The tissue was malignant.

It was all downhill after that. She had a double mastectomy. When I asked the surgeon if he got it all he replied, "Cancer is treatable, but not curable."

Pastor June, I couldn't take it. I couldn't watch her suffer. Nothing cut the pain. She was patient and endured so much. I tried to control my drinking and got home as soon as I could after school to be with her. The children took turns coming and that seemed to comfort her, but they were all involved in their own families and careers, and I suspect it depressed them to see her like that.

It was in June. School was over for the summer. I still had to go to the office every day, but the pressures were less than when the term was underway. When I was able to concentrate on my work, I managed to blur the edge a little so it didn't cut so sharp, but this fateful night, I couldn't deny it any longer. I came home and started to drink. If she could take drugs to numb her pain, why couldn't I numb mine?

I went into her room and stood by her bed. She still was beautiful, even though the cancer had hollowed her cheeks and robbed her of flesh. You have to believe me. When she said it, her voice was nearly inaudible. I didn't know if I heard her correctly. She repeated it.

"The pills. Get me out of this. Help me. If you love me, get the pills."

It took the liquor, the passion of her request, and my own inability to face this one day longer to act on her request. I moved in a trance toward the table where her prescriptions stood. Mechanically, I emptied one of the bottles into her mouth, pill by pill, determined to love her beyond all this into eternity. Then, I sat down and emptied my own bottle. I passed out in the chair next to her bed.

The birds woke me up at dawn. Sarah Jane was on the bed, peaceful and serene on the white sheets. Gradually I realized that she was dead. She was cold when I touched her. Suddenly, I remembered the night before. I remembered what I did. I killed her.

In panic I ran from the house, took nothing with me, got into the car and fled. I never went back. I drove and drove and drove. When I reached southern Oregon, I sold the car and tore up my driver's license. From that moment, I assumed a series of aliases, finally becoming just "Lenny."

I continued to run and hide. My shame and guilt covered all that I did. I hitch-hiked, rode freight cars, slept in alleys, and numbed my conscience with booze.

Last year, I came to Seattle. I always liked university communities, and here I found street men who accepted me without asking many questions. So many wanderers came in and out of the area that the police didn't give me any trouble. I stayed clean and neat, folded into the group so I didn't stand out, and managed to hold my liquor so no one realized I wasn't truly sober.

Not a day went by that I didn't miss my lovely Sarah Jane. The boys tired of hearing me reminisce about the good days. I told them she died of cancer. Now I am telling you that I took her life before cancer had the last word.

I am a felon. I am wanted by the law. My children exhausted every known avenue to track me and finally came to believe that I too had died. In a way, they were right. My soul collapsed and seeped away, leaving me empty and afraid that night that she died. I never found life again. These years of existence on the streets betrayed all that I knew and cared about.

I want to thank you and the people of the church for allowing me to come in out of the rain, so to speak. The last bit of dignity I knew was when the members of the porch patrol came by and invited me to pray with them. I hadn't been able to pray. I thought God would crush me if I said his name. At first, I covered my ears so I wouldn't hear what they said. But

*one night, the Spirit drew close to me
and I said God, not in fear and dread,
but as though I was talking to a friend
who understood and forgave.*

*As you read these words, I know
more than you do. I am on the other
side now. You still sit believing in
what you can't see.*

Bless you, Lenny

Chapter Eleven

PATRICK

Only Patrick and Patch John were on the porch when I stopped by to visit. Patrick was talkative. He told of his times at sea when he worked on a fishing boat in Alaska. He dreamed of someday going back, but an infection in his toes led to their amputation, and he couldn't balance on deck anymore. Now, he walked with a cane.

He had trimmed his hair, and a red edge of beard decorated his chin. Under other circumstances, he might have appeared strikingly handsome, but now a hard light beamed from the sailor's shipwrecked eyes, and hunger and drink shadowed the curves of his fine facial structure.

On nights like this one, he entertained us with his Irish charm. He was a storyteller. Patch John and I sat hypnotized as his voice rose and fell, now whispering, now roaring like the elements that struck on the night he lost his toes.

"I'd been in those waters through the worst of everything. Storms flew in our face in an instant, blowing from a soft breeze to a mighty whelp. We were way out there with nothing to hide behind; our closest companions the whales and the dolphins, the sea birds, and celestial signs. We charted by the stars. You don't know what lonesome is until you've been six months at sea. To protect our souls, we learned to pull inside when the lonely hours and boredom covered us.

"But when the fierce times hit, we automatically came together, willing toward one thing: survival.

"I thought I'd seen it all until that night. It was the night I dropped out of the universe. There were no stars. There were no clear sounds, only sounds howling inside of sounds. Echoes of voices seducing us toward the rocks. The boards on deck cried salty tears of anguish as they strained to return to the tall timbers on land. They had carried enough. High in the branches of the forest, the winds played a song that tore apart the heart of the craft, loosened its bolts and drove it to a frenzy of exhausted surrender.

"It was so dark and wild. My arm reached toward Mort, my closest mate, but before I could grab hold. he disappeared in the waves. Behind me, gagging and thrashing, Tom choked on his own vomit and sank beneath the sea.

"Instinctively, I caught onto a large board and pulled myself up from the freezing cold. My legs and feet were numb. I was alone without any living creature. I passed into deep sleep, expecting never to wake again. There were no words, only the stirrings of the Spirit that knew my yearnings and lifted my prayer beyond my strength to think or speak it.

"I opened my eyes to the light of dawn. The monstrous upheaval from the hurricane force winds was replaced by calm. A horny whistle sounded from a boat, washed in golden sunlight, that mystically drifted toward me. I waved to demonstrate that I was alive! Someone got the signal. I kept my life, but I lost my toes. Yet, in another way, my life was the sea and without my toes that life was gone. That was my last voyage. I came here to the Vets hospital, and I've been adrift since, asking why I didn't go with Mort and Tom.

"Sometimes I think I have to find Rita again to figure that question out. She owned the WHALE SPOUT CAFÉ in Kodiak. I never missed going straight there when we put in to dock. Sometimes I'd even step into the kitchen and mix up a pot of chowder or tend the tables if it got busy. Her man went off with another woman and she had to cook up a new life.

"Her red hair was shiny as a salmon skin and her spunk as slippery. But behind her crystal blue eyes there was a search going on, and when she flashed her grin, she fetched me to it. We were both looking for a place to plant our feet.

"I guess I loved her but I didn't figure it out in time. She left Kodiak with no forwarding address. She saved money for a plane ticket to Anchorage, closed her café, and disappeared. I think I'm getting ready to go find her."

The boys thought themselves most clever when they snatched a phrase of Gaelic from Patrick and tossed it into the air as though they had mastered the language. Drunk on wine, they named Patrick their saint. On St. Patrick's Day, they bought a can of Spam and a head of cabbage, put a green paper halo on Patrick's head, and escorted him to the park for a celebration.

"Finest corned beef we could afford," they said, as they took the magic key to open the Spam can.

Patrick recalled the party as we sat on the steps hearing the traffic go by on 50th. "At least you could have cooked the cabbage!" Patrick reflected.

Patch John laughed. Patrick always helped him to laugh. That night, Patrick was spinning dreams that seemed viable. When I left, he was talking like a man with plans to leave the porch, but later that night, he happened down the wrong alley and was jumped by a gang. They beat him unmercifully. Somehow, early in the morning, he stumbled up the hill to the church and collapsed.

It was Saturday. A crew of volunteers was working on the church lawn. Martin came around the corner dragging cut branches and was surprised to see a man crumpled in a corner of the porch. Usually, no one was there in the daytime. Martin was on the porch patrol, and when he came up the steps to get a closer look, he recognized Patrick.

"What happened?" he blurted out, seeing Patrick's painful expression and swollen face. "Did someone attack you?"

"I'm okay. I just need to rest," Patrick said softly.

"I think I should get you to the emergency room," Martin answered.

"No. No ambulance. Just let me be a while," Patrick answered.

"Will you go if I take you and stay with you?" Martin persisted.

Wincing, Patrick nodded, unable to withstand the unbearable shocks of pain that radiated through his shoulder and side.

"I'll be right back. Help is on the way!" Martin said in a tone of reassuring comfort.

Martin did as he had promised. The son of a Lutheran pastor, he was familiar with people in pain. He chose not to follow his father's footsteps, and became an engineer instead. But although ministry wasn't his career choice, compassion and caring remained a large part of his character. He did not abandon Patrick. He waited for hours in the emergency waiting room. He expected that the nurse would tell him that Patrick had been admitted, so was surprised when Patrick appeared in a cast that covered his entire right side.

Patrick wanted to go back to University Lutheran, and he did. The boys took turns getting him food, feeding him, and helping him down the hill to the bathroom in the park. Most of the time, he lay on his blankets on the porch, trying to keep his spirits up while his body healed. It took months.

The neighbors had not dropped their efforts. They called the Bishop again and requested that he intervene. They called the health department and requested that it fine the church. They claimed the men were a threat to children because of their unkempt appearance, drinking, and vulgarity, and demanded that the daycare center license be revoked. The pressure was on.

The spring that Patrick suffered the attack, there was a drug bust in a vacant house across from the church. The neighborhood concentrated their efforts on our porch, ignoring the activities over there. The house in question was abandoned by an absentee landlord who had little interest in the area. Runaway kids had been living there illegally, and the police finally closed in to flush them out. 50th, a major east-west thoroughfare, was blocked off to all traffic for several hours.

It was around ten o'clock in the evening, and Patrick was alone on the porch. A police officer crossed 50th, came on church property, and ordered Patrick to evacuate. Patrick said he had permission to be there, but when he couldn't produce any verification of that or direct the policeman to someone in the building to back his claim, he was forced to get up and go.

"We are clearing the entire area," he was told. It was the end of Lent, the time in the liturgical year when Jesus comes into the city triumphant, is judged, and condemned to the cross. Still in his cast, Patrick struggled to get down the hill alone on that stormy night of Holy Week.

In the throes of all the extra liturgies, hospital calls, and the reactions to the drug bust, I lost track of Patrick, assuming that he had gone with the others to another place until things quieted down.

When the congregation gathered for Good Friday services, there were two screens at the front of the darkened sanctuary. Jim Haney, architect and accomplished photographer, had agreed to help me develop the order of worship.

Famous paintings of Christ's passion were shown alongside candid shots of the boys on the porch, street kids, and other homeless people in the U. District.

Jim photographed and interviewed them, combining them with the Good Friday story. The final slide was of Patrick, sitting on the church porch in his body cast, smiling and lifting his hand in the sign of peace.

Norm Twist, a captain in the Seattle fire department, read the Passion account.

Strange how connections are made. The next morning, he was assigned to the firehouse at the bottom of the hill below the church. The captain regularly in charge was taken ill and so Norm was sent over to fill in for the weekend.

An emergency call came in at 7:00 a.m. Saturday morning. Soon after, my home phone rang, and when I answered I recognized Norm's voice.

"Good morning, Pastor. I'm not sure, but I think I have some information you would want. We just picked up a dead man in a body cast at Sojourner Park. He died sometime during the night. I am wondering if it's the same man in the slide who gave us the peace sign last night at worship. First name is Patrick. Last name Major."

I was stunned, shaken to the point of tears. Then a stream of questions: Who found him? What caused his death? Where is the body? Is there any family? Was he attacked or beaten? Was he all alone?

"I can't really answer. His buddies found him on a bench. He's been taken to the county coroner's office. Maybe they can tell you more."

I immediately called the coroner's office. They were in the process of tracing family members. An autopsy would be done to determine the cause of death. At this point, it did not appear that he had suffered any further violence.

It was that between-time. The day between Good Friday and Easter morning. The time of suspension between the total darkness of death and the rising light of Easter life. The time Jesus descended into hell.

I anguished during those hours. Could it have been different had I been in my office to intervene with the police or if someone had stopped by to see him and called for medical help? If we had rented a motel room so he had a safe, warm place, someone with him to comfort and attend to his needs? Should one of us have taken him into our home?

Patrick deserved to die in a better place, not on a hard bench by a public toilet in an urban park. He should have died better than he had been forced to live.

I dressed and went in search of the boys. None of them was on the porch, so I walked the length of the Ave, behind the supermarket, the playground in the vacant school yard, past the Vietnamese store where they lined up to buy cheap wine ... and could not find any of them.

Disappointed, I turned to go up the hill to the church. Someone behind me said in a stage whisper, "Pastor June, did you know that Patrick died?"

It was Patch John, sitting in the doorway of a vacant restaurant on the corner. He had been drinking. His face was wet with tears. He was hiding like a wounded animal. Dazed, he looked at me as one who might understand the pain and shock of this morning's loss.

"Me and Teardrop and Wolfman found Patrick with part of his coat over his head, so we thought we'd let him sleep. We had a bottle of wine, so we went down to drink that and get Patrick some breakfast. When we went back to wake him up, Teardrop noticed that his stomach wasn't moving. I told Wolfman to take the coat off his face. His face was the color of ashes. His lips were blue. I ran to the market and called 911, but he was dead." Patch John wept. "We had some good times together, him and I."

I sat down in the doorway beside Patch John and held his hand. I wondered aloud how it would be without Patrick. Both of us knew it would not be the same.

"I knew he wasn't feeling so good," Patch John said. "Ever since he took the beating, he got weak and lost his interest in things. He quit telling us stories. It knocked his spirits. I sure didn't expect to find him dead when we got back. Guess he was dead when we found him and we didn't even know it."

His body heaved with grief. Patrick had been a friend. Patch John didn't have many of those. What was more, death came suddenly and very close. Would he be next?

Chapter Twelve

EASTER

aster dawned. The church filled. Outside, rain clouds spilled torrents on fancy dresses and tailored suits, as people dashed inside from the parking lot. Like wet puppies, they stood in the hallway shaking off excess moisture, chattering against the backdrop of trumpets blasting in the sanctuary. Not even thunder and lightning could compete with the sounds from the choir, the instruments, the congregation singing, *Christ the Lord is Risen Today, Hallelujah!*

My heart remained heavy as I stepped into the pulpit to preach. I began, "There has been a death."

Quiet settled over the people. I felt sure that some thought I was thinking back to the cross and Christ's crucifixion. That was where we had left each other on Good Friday evening. Others braced for news that someone from the congregation had suddenly died. Only a few recognized the name of Patrick Major or why there should be particular attention paid to him.

Something of the same grief and confusion that the Marys felt when they came weeping early the first Easter morning, threatened to rise up in my voice. I took a deep breath and continued.

"Patrick, like Jesus, was a marginal man. He owned no property. He rented no place of business. His skills were not so unique that he could not be replaced. He was despised and rejected by many. At the end, only three friends stood by. They went to get him breakfast and returned to find him dead.

"A concrete public toilet became Patrick's tomb. Like poets, visionaries, mystics, and messengers, Patrick daily faced the question of who he was in a world that did not understand him. He was seen as another useless mouth to feed, another man overboard! In this utilitarian age, which pushes out onto the fringe everyone who is considered nonproductive, Patrick had no place to lay his head.

"He wandered onto our church steps, seeking sanctuary. He was met by a band of Christians who came at night to visit with him, pray with him, and give comfort and encouragement. Members of the porch patrol from our household of faith.

"The last glimpse we had of Patrick was at the Good Friday services. In the closing slide, he lifted his eyes in hope and raised his hand to give us the sign of peace. Sometime during that night, he died. And now I say, peace be with you, Patrick. It is Easter morning and we have come to celebrate resurrection.

"There will be a memorial service for Patrick in Sojourner Park where he died, Tuesday at 5:00 p.m. All are invited. It is to those like Patrick that the Lord Jesus comes. He looks upon their adversity and brings them out of their troubles.

"There is a twist to all of this. We go to the porch assuming that the men there are the sick ones and we are the well ones. We look with contempt or with pity on their addictions. Yet, it occurs to me that the men on the porch have come to US. To open our eyes to see our own addiction, our own need for recovery. They visit us as angels unaware, sent to roll the stone away that blocks the door to our future in the city. They come as truth, and only when we know them will we be free to be full participants in humanity.

"Their sickness is obvious. Our sickness is elusive. We suppose that we are safe, secure, and immune to all suffering, that we can avoid confronting it by posting signs on the entrance or writing a check to a rescue mission downtown.

"But God has loved us so much, He has sent us witnesses, has given us a live opportunity to grow beyond the borders of our own tradition and class, to find healing through relationship and compassion. As the gap between the pews and the porch widens, we become more vulnerable, more afraid, and more protective.

"The boys live and die in the open air of the city streets, while we suffocate behind electric alarm systems and locks and chains to seal our homes.

"We are in as much need of redemption as the men on our porch. We are in need of healing, just as they are. The power of Easter levels the ground, removes the stones that block our way, to open a future we cannot yet imagine. Salvation knocks. Let all enter. Let all be made whole. One bread, one body, one Lord of all. AMEN."

After both services, people left the church to find leaflets on their windshields. At first, they thought it was an invitation to a restaurant for Easter brunch.

~ ~ ~ ~ ~ ~

AN EASTER NOTICE

(A scan of the actual notice can be viewed at the end of the book. This notice was retyped verbatim for the sake of legibility.)

Dear Members of the Congregation of the University Lutheran Church (ULC) :

The neighbors of your church are distributing this note with the hope that as a congregation, you can influence the course of action that your pastor is following. The single-family homeowners and others have tried to reason with the ULC leadership, without success.

The situation has deteriorated to the extent that the University District Community Council (UDCC) is requesting city enforcement for a public health menace.

This is what we face on a daily basis:

1) Drunken men are sleeping on the church steps, porches, and in the bushes. They urinate, defecate, and vomit on the church grounds, Their litter is empty wine bottles, trash, and used toilet paper. We have taken one hypodermic needle from the steps near the curb on 16th NE. We have photos for documentation.

2) The men have begun going into neighborhood yards to relieve themselves.

3) The men have harassed children and adults.

4) Most recently, a man was observed masturbating during the day by one of the preschool teachers.

In January, a letter from the church was written to the neighborhood that distorted the facts. The number of sleeping and drunk men, and the amount of filth outside of the church is steadily increasing despite the claim to the opposite.

The church's neighbors should not be its victims. It is **misguided** Christian charity which condones the activities listed above. **Real** Christian charity would provide drug rehabilitation, a proper facility, supervision, and indoor toilets. Please, please call your ULC council members and tell them that you do **not** want your church to be this neighborhood's cesspool.

Thank you.
Signed by neighborhood families

On University Lutheran Church letterhead
(A scan of the actual letter can be viewed at the end of the book. This notice was retyped verbatim for the sake of legibility)

April 14, 1993

Dear Neighbors and Members of University Lutheran:

Over the past months, we have provided a temporary sanctuary for a few men who have come looking for a peaceful place. They are alcoholics. They are in need of all the things you listed in the leaflet distributed on Easter Sunday. The city is not providing adequate safe shelter, treatment, or a clear invitation to recovery. Once rehabilitated, there are no jobs, no housing, no encouragement.

There are people in the building from early morning to around 10 PM each night. No one has complained about a "cesspool." Our grounds are kept well. Our porch is closely monitored. It is our property. Teams of our members have faithfully gone to the porch. We have kept a log and monitored alcohol use, the condition of the porch, and general behavior. When our visitors have become sick on our place, we have taken the responsibility to clean it up.

Nothing would indicate that the needle you referred to belonged to the men on our porch. Hundreds of people pass by our corner. We are across the street from the squat which the police raided recently, not far from fraternity row, and only a few blocks above the Ave.

No report was filed with us by the day-care that a man was masturbating in front of their staff member. None of us has witnessed such behavior, Should that occur on our property, we would, of course, address the problem. .

It is our hope that your letter indicates concern, not just about our small effort to meet human need, but about a growing awareness of the critical nature of the social changes that are happening in the district.

We will join you in your community efforts to provide rehabilitation, a proper facility, supervision, and indoor toilets. We admit that our efforts are inadequate and would welcome a combined cooperative effort that invites all segments of the University District to find humane, just solutions to these difficult situations.

The sooner we come up with alternatives, the sooner our porch people will move.

Signed by Members of the University Lutheran Church Council

The charges backfired. Instead of engendering support, the neighbors lost credibility. The next day, parents of the daycare children called a meeting to support the porch men. They recognized that the tactics were dirty and the accusations unfounded.

Tuesday, in Sojourner Park where Patrick died, a proper memorial service was held. The gathering was a strange configuration of folks. Word had traveled. Faces of those who lived on the streets formed the core. About twenty from the congregation came. A delegation of Baptists, noted for their social conscience, huddled on the far side. Curious onlookers, who just happened to be passing through the park, lingered and participated.

The assistant to the Bishop, who did nothing official but expressed a heart for the matter, decided to be in solidarity with the cause.

Hanging on the limb of a strong, tall tree was a cross made of feathers, acorns, twigs, and flowers. Wolfman had created it from natural materials in the park.

Teardrop wailed uncontrollably, soon joined by Patch John, bent with grief as he

Article from *The Daily*, the University of Washington student newspaper (photos / text by Dan Schlatter):

Friends grieve over homeless man's death

A small gathering collected in Cowen Park last Thursday to commemorate the life of a friend and a brother.

Patrick Michael Meehan, 42, was found dead on a bench in Cowen Park early last week.

Meehan, who often spent the night in the park, was found in the morning by a fellow street person named Rodney. "I went to feel his pulse and his hand was like ice," Rodney said.

Meehan apparently died of alcohol-related ailments.

Many of the 40 or so people who gathered to remember Meehan were members of University Lutheran Church.

The church is involved with the homeless, having formed what they call the "porch patrol" back in September. The group helps keep an eye out for street people who often spend the night on the church's front steps.

Meehan was remembered by many as a kind-hearted, gentle person.

Pastor June Nilssen of University Lutheran Church said to the group, "Whenever you said good-bye to Patrick, he would always say, "Walk softly with God in your heart."

Meehan was born in Ireland and grew up in California. He was a sergeant in the Marine Corps and served more than 18 months in Vietnam between 1967 and 1969.

He had lived on the streets and been an alcoholic for many years.

Patrick Meehan (1951-1993).

A group of friends met in Cowen Park to remember Patrick Meehan. One of Meehan's close friends, "Teardrop," leads the group out of the park to University Lutheran Church, where the remembrance continued.

read the 23rd Psalm. Bert, from church, played his guitar and led us in singing *Amazing Grace*. Voices in the crowd gave testimony to how fine a friend Patrick had been and how much he would be missed on the streets. Hugs and peace were passed. By then, about fifty people had gathered.

Wolfman's cross was taken from the tree branch and carried at the front of a procession that solemnly moved up the street past the neighbor's houses. Silently, when we arrived at the church, we assembled on the lawn by the porch.

Jim Haney had carved a small, simple wooden cross with Patrick's name and the date of his death, which he now hung above the corner where Patrick often slept, as a marker commemorating the last days of his life.

"Acknowledge, we humbly beseech you," I prayed, "a sheep of your own fold, a lamb of your own flock, a sinner of your own redeeming. Receive Patrick into the blessed rest of everlasting peace and the glorious company of the saints in light."

Then Patch John took his place at the center of the steps to announce that he had brought a package of Oreo cookies for a small reception on the lawn. He tore open the wrappings and passed them, like consecrated food, to share among the gathered. Instead of breaking bread, we broke the color line: chocolate on one side, vanilla on the other, stuck together with the sweet filling of comfort and mercy.

Chapter Thirteen

MOTHER'S DAY

Midnight in Portland can be raw and wet. The night John stopped to get egg rolls after a movie was one of those chilling times. His favorite Chinese take-out spot beamed like a lighthouse in the storm as he dashed through puddles to get there before it closed. Led by the tangy smell of egg rolls, he pushed his way through the door, and startled a small group of men clustered toward the back of the restaurant. Suddenly, blinding energy split open his eyes. He had been shot. Bloody and stunned, he struggled to get up and was shot again, this time in his leg.

"I seen something I shouldnta saw," he told me later.

His world shifted into slow motion as lights, officers, white coats, and sirens swirled above him, and he was sucked down into a hole of black unconsciousness. He was accused of robbery. There was not enough evidence to make a case, but he was scared, because he could identify two of the men he caught in the middle of a drug deal. It didn't help that he was black.

He left Portland for the streets of Seattle. He drank, too much. One of the bullets had lodged near his brain and where there had been a soulful brown eye, there was now an empty socket that he covered with a patch. Shattered, he built solidarity with his new brothers on the street. They never used their real names, so they called him Patch John.

One night, he found our church porch. It felt safe. He listened to the rain. The night wind was sharp and cold. That porch became home for three years. Wrapped in blankets, warmed by wine, he whispered into the holy darkness, "God, thank you."

But things worsened for Patch John after Patrick died. He moved to the doorstep on the alley at the back of the church. He was there alone. Even when it grew very cold, he refused to go to a shelter. The night finally came when he was found delirious on the Ave and taken to the detox center downtown.

When he sobered up, he faithfully promised that he would go for extended treatment. He showed me a slip with an appointment for evaluation, a telephone number, and a contact person.

Mother's Day, at the 11 o'clock service, I glanced down from the chancel to see Patch John come in with a "friend." I had no idea who this "friend" might be. His head was completely shaved, like a refugee from a Nazi concentration camp. The two of them sat in the front pew directly beneath the pulpit.

The church was full. Mothers wore corsages and elegant dresses, while their families attended them in equally fine attire. Bouquets of flowers festooned the altar. Mother's Day is a special time for families to reunite and pay homage to the matriarch. Black Patch John and his bald companion just didn't fit the picture.

During the sermon hymn, Patch John rose and walked up to stand next to me in front of the congregation.

He leaned over and whispered, "Pastor June, I have to speak."

"Have you been drinking?" I whispered back.

"Just the early morning fix."

I pointed to the verse we were singing and extended the book. He declined.

"Who is the guy with you?" I sang into his ear.

"That's Wolfman."

WOLFMAN? Before, his shaggy eyebrows had hung over his eyes. From the top of his head to the nape of his neck, he had been all hair.

"What happened?"

"Critters. His scalp got sores. Had to shave him."

The hymn ended. I motioned for everyone to sit down, and then returned to the pulpit to announce that Patch John, one of the residents on the church porch, had an important message to deliver. When I stepped aside and let him have the microphone, there was an audible sound throughout the sanctuary.

Patch John took charge. He held up the paper that said he was to report in the morning for extended treatment.

"I want to personally thank the members of the congregation who have supported and encouraged me and the others. I think of Jim Haney, Clarence Pankowsky (hope I got that one right!) Mary Post, Grace Updown, Jack Brigstone, Joyce James, Martin, guess I don't know your last name, Beth, the mime who entertains us sometimes, Bert and Pastor June ... people on the porch patrol. In the morning, I am going to the detox center. This slip of paper tells the time of my appointment. Keep prayin' for me, okay?"

I took my place next to him, thanked him, and directed him to the front pew to sit with Wolfman, now turned skinhead. Anticipating the next crisis, Clarence and Jack came forward to see that they didn't drink all the wine in the common cup.

As I broke the bread and distributed it to those kneeling at the rail, I smelled Zest soap strong and clean, the overpowering fragrance of expensive seductive perfume, after-shave lotion, sweaty underarm odors from one of our adolescent confirmands, and the smell of rot-gut booze from the unwashed bodies of Patch John and Wolfman.

The broken bread was sanctified by the words, "This is my body, given for you. Take eat. Do this in remembrance of me."

Humanity on our knees, broken and hungry. One place where we were all equal. Where words of grace and mercy gave each of us voice and identity. Where we could freely confess that much of the afflictions we suffered were brought about by the decisions and actions we ourselves blamed others for.

Surrounded at the coffee hour by congratulatory well-wishers, Patch John repeated his intentions to be sober for life.

The next morning, he lay drunk in the alley at the back of the church. He had failed the wake-up call and missed the sacred appointment. When I spotted him, I decided to let him sleep it off. The guy had the lives of an alley cat. I figured he was on the eighth, and wondered if he would get the picture before he struck out in the ninth.

My appointment with the organist shifted my focus to more ethereal matters. He was at the keyboard playing Bach. Patch John lay beyond the window within earshot of the same magnificent music. Perhaps he would awaken, hear *Jesu, Joy of Man's Desiring*, and think he had gone to heaven. I imagined him saying, "You know, Jesu, my joy would be even fuller if we had a bottle of wine."

Patch John pulled me back to my seminary training, when as an intern in the municipal court in Springfield, Ohio, I had dealt with a continuous parade of drunks who filed past the judge over to the Clark County jail. I learned to recognize them all. Round and round the turnstile swung, as they staggered over from court, dried out overnight, and got dumped back onto the streets in the morning. Invariably, their bodies would crave a drink, and the police would be on the lookout for them. Like a diabetic in need of insulin, they would go for the bottle, drink themselves unconscious, and end up back in jail.

In my naiveté, I thought a pot of homemade soup would fix things. Sam, a regular, had tremors so bad he couldn't hold a pen to sign his discharge papers. He was a sick man and needed medical attention, not incarceration. But there were no provisions for treatment, and the judge insisted he had no alternative but to release him.

That night, I found Sam's house and stood knocking on the door, holding a hot bucket of fresh vegetable soup. I was about to leave when I heard something or someone fall down a flight of steps.

"Oh, my God!" I gasped as the door slowly creaked open and Sam gazed up at me from the hallway floor.

"Are you okay?" I asked.

"Always, sweetheart, always," he mumbled.

"I brought soup," I said feebly, realizing how drunk he was.

"Bring it on up, sweetie," he said, crawling up the steps, whistling *She'll be comin' round the mountain when she comes.*

The place was small. A door opened into a bathroom right off the kitchen. A circle of assorted broken chairs—all different— surrounded a round, plastic-topped table loaded with empty wine bottles. Through an open archway, I saw a heap of six bodies—all my clients from jail—lying on a bed, bare-chested, their pants unzipped, and their shoes kicked off into a pile on the linoleum. Their combined snores had the deafening rumble of the percussion section of the Cincinnati symphony. What a hopeless heap of pickled flesh! I wanted to leave and never turn back.

"Have you got anything I can pour this into?" I asked, instead.

"You betcha! Here's two empty milk cartons somebody left," he answered, retrieving them from the trash.

"No pans?" I asked.

"Don't know. I just got the place last night."

I rinsed the cartons and poured the soup into them, imagining the gang each taking a swig like it was wine from a bottle. With all my idealism, I still couldn't trust leaving my pan.

Chapter Fourteen

"LORD, TO WHOM SHALL WE GO?"

Sunshine kissed the puckered waters of the ship canal as I strolled over the University Bridge. Small craft purred and sputtered on their way to the locks and the larger Sound, as tiny leaves uncurled to embrace the bursting buds of spring.

I loved walking to work on such mornings, and stopped midpoint to lift my arms in tribute to the immense energy of the new season. Mountains, trees, waters, and all that moved in them, lifted their praises to exalt a God who never quits creating. The wheels of the season turned, pouring luscious, flowery fragrances into the air so potent they overwhelmed the fumes of the cars and buses that growled and wheezed in the morning traffic.

Once over the bridge, I cut through to the Ave. It was a two-mile hike from my house to the church. Things were quiet. The Flamingo had opened its sidewalk tables, and a few hearty souls pretended it was warm enough to actually enjoy sitting there. A sliver of sunlight reflected from the windows of a disco club, beaming assurance that today, at least, the rains would keep their distance. It was a morning when the Kingdom of God felt in my hands. Close. Intimate. Tangible.

Standing at the curb, waiting for the signal to change, I smiled at the small, Oriental man standing alongside me. At first, he looked sour and grim.

"Good morning," I said. "Isn't it beautiful today?"

To my absolute delight, his face opened like a rose. "It is indeed," he responded. "Thank you for reminding me."

We crossed and went our separate ways. The dinghy storefronts were washed in golden light. It was early for much activity in the stores. I decided to indulge in a croissant and got in line at the newsstand. There was Tom Hagan, a graduate student at the university, who lived a few doors from the church and came occasionally to worship.

"Good morning," he said. "What was going on at your place last night?"

"You mean at University Lutheran?" I asked.

"Yeah. There were cops all over the place. They woke me up around four this morning. I walked past there, but I couldn't get any take on what it was all about."

"Were there medics there?" I asked.

"No. I didn't see any. Just police."

"I guess I better skip the croissant and hike up the hill," I said.

This whole business was madness. As soon as I stepped into Hope's office, I was told to go downstairs to see Cary Ferguson, director of the daycare. The window in the girls' lavatory had been smashed. Glass was splattered all over the floor. Cary had a broom in her hand, preparing to sweep up the mess. She said there had been a robbery around 4:00 a.m. The police had interrupted four masked teenagers apparently trying to pry open the office door upstairs. (Did spring also bring out aggressive hormones in teenagers?)

"Believe me, I was shocked when I walked in early this morning and found all this broken glass," Cary continued. "I went to call the police and was told they had already been here. So, I went to the porch to see if the guys out there knew anything. They were all sitting up, wide awake for a change.

"Loose started right in telling me what happened. He had to go to the toilet, so about 3:30 a.m., when he was heading for the bushes, he saw moving shadows inside the hallway of the church. At first, he thought it was a bad dream or the effects of last night's bottle. But as he listened, his instincts told him there was a robbery in progress. He said he jiggled Patch John's arm for a reality check. They agreed that someone was definitely at work in there and if it had been legitimate, they wouldn't be carrying flash-lights and rushing about in a frenzy. So Loose took off down the hill to call 911 on the pay phone. Within minutes, a police car arrived in the parking lot and Loose and Patch John met them there to report what they had seen."

I got the rest of the story from the police report. The door from the parking lot was secure, as were all the other entrances. Before the police could enter the building, the kids crashed out of the door by the organ and started to run for it. They didn't get far! All four had stayed overnight in the teen shelter in our church basement, which was open one night a week. Volunteers knew them by name.

They were street kids looking for computers, silver candleholders, stereos: anything that would bring them drug money. One kid was only 13. He was the kid I saw with the pet rat under his shirt. The oldest was 17, still considered a minor though he operated like he was in his forties. Trish was the only girl. She came along because the fourth member was her boyfriend. She was 15; he was chronologically 19, but emotionally just a dumb kid.

Cary was shaken by the whole episode. The daycare's new computer was returned somewhat damaged. It wasn't favorable public relations with the parents of the children. They would be alarmed. She repeated, over and over, that Loose and Patch John were the heroes. "If they hadn't acted, who knows how the building would have been trashed!"

When I talked to Loose and Patch John, they said the worst part for them was that those few kids returned theft for the hospitality they had been given.

"Pastor June," Patch John said, "This is our place. We watch out for things. You folks have been good to us. You're like family. Nobody is going to rob or hurt you as long as we have anything to say about it."

I believed him.

* * * * *

Marvin Olson had an itch in his britches, and he was declaring his discomfort to everyone but me. I called him and said I planned to come over to talk, but he insisted that he come to my office instead.

I had heard via the grapevine that he was upset because I didn't agree to baptize his twin daughters' babies. I assumed this was the major issue that disturbed him, but when the conversation opened, he denied that he had any problems with that.

"The baptism thing is water over the dam. I got that sorted out with my daughters," he said.

"But you are upset about something, aren't you?" I continued.

"I don't really think you want to hear about it," he said, looking out the window.

"Oh, yes, I do. Tell me. I like things out in the open."

"All right. What is really eating at me is you're a woman. Didn't St. Paul say women should keep silent?"

He took me by surprise with that one. "Yes. Go on," I coaxed him.

"And another thorn is that voice of yours. Have you ever thought of taking speech classes to lower the pitch? It drives me crazy to sit every Sunday and hear you chanting the liturgy and preaching from the pulpit. I do not approve of women taking authority over men. Who knows what kind of influence you have with the women."

For at least ten minutes, he berated my role as a spiritual leader, ending with the scandalous tolerance I promoted for the drunks on the stoop.

"It is a disgrace to have those no-good freeloaders on public display on our corner. And now, the robbery! This is the last straw! Them trying to break into the office! The neighbors have every right to complain," he shouted. "It would be best for everyone if you just resigned."

I took a long, deep breath before I answered him.

"Marvin, it was four teenage kids who broke into the building. The men on the porch got the police here. You've got the whole story wrong. Further, I could take all the voice lessons in the world and still not learn how to talk bass. I'm a woman. And I happen to be the pastor called to serve this congregation. The people here invited me, and I am not finished with what I came to do. You obviously are not having a good worship experience here anymore. If I am a block for you and you can't find God in this place, I suggest you transfer."

"We just come here because we have friends we like to go to dinner with once a month," he grumbled.

"Well, then," I replied, "go somewhere else to worship and see your friends for dinner once a month! Now, wasn't that easy?"

He got up reluctantly, refused my outstretched hand, and said, "I'm sorry, but you'll never convince me that a woman should wear a collar!"

When he left, I felt wounded and somewhat abused.

Yet, maybe he was right. Maybe I wasn't adequate for this position. At least he had the courage to come in and face me. How many others with whom "he went to dinner with once a month" were saying the same things, but not to me?

I sat on the sofa in silence, waiting for the Spirit of God to move my feelings into words. I was tired and confused. Then, from a wellspring of residual weariness, prayer rose to my lips.

"Lord, do I love you as you would have me love you? If I am wrong in my stand with the boys and need to change, show me the next steps. Help me remember that this is your ministry. I am called to follow your will.

Forgive me, I know there are many opinions, and mine is not always the right one. Open my ears to listen. Support me in my struggles and pour your love into my heart. I am so tired. Please, renew my strength..."

The prayer was interrupted by a loud banging on the door. I opened to Wolfman, who stood puffing at the threshold.

"Pastor June, I just ran up the hill to tell you that they took Patch John to University Hospital. He's bad. Real bad. Can you go to see him?"

* * * * *

It was early morning the next day. The blinds in the hospital room were closed so only dim light filtered through. Patch John was writhing on the bed, his hands tied to the metal sides that were pulled up to keep him from falling out. His lips opened and closed as he sucked an imaginary bottle. Occasionally, his tongue protruded like a white-coated sponge between his purple lips.

As his body twisted and fought to get free, his glazed eye stared straight at me. I knew he could not see me, yet his gaze penetrated like an ultrasound beam.

My mind imaged the body of my own father ravaged by alcohol, lying in a hospital bed with blocks propped under the bed's legs to keep his vital signs stable. Daddy, a brilliant attorney, leader in the state legislature, candidate for Congress, was sitting up, pouring an imaginary shot of whiskey into a glass that didn't exist except in his hallucinations. Atrophy of the brain, the physicians named it. That was what caused him to parade naked, except for his favorite felt hat on his head, outdoors in the backyard of the family home that fateful morning when Mother called us to come home and help!

The police had to put my father in a strait jacket to get him into an ambulance and drive him 200 miles to the experts at University Hospital, Minneapolis.

Tears flooded my cheeks as Patch John screamed and groaned. I had seen DTs before and had stood helpless by the bed watching the destructive last chapters of this addiction. This disease! I envisioned finding Patch John as I found my father, dead on the garage floor with a high count of alcohol in his blood.

So that was it then? Was I still trying to save my father? Was that what goaded me to tramp around to hospitals and alleys and porch steps trying to intervene? Was I still trying to rescue Daddy, buried so many years ago in the scorching sun of summer?

It was an important connection, no question about it. The resurgence of pain such memories triggered was real. But the man lying before me was real, too. I came out of love for Patch John.

"John. You are a good man. You are a young man. Oh, God! Is there no hope for you?" I whispered aloud.

I was startled to hear the voice of a nurse who had entered the room without my noticing.

"I'm afraid it doesn't look very promising. The liver damage is heavy. He's on his way to Veteran's Hospital. This won't be an easy time of it. What's your relationship to the patient?"

"I'm his pastor," I said without hesitation.

"Good! This one's going to need a lot of prayer. It'll take a miracle," the nurse said as she tightened the straps around his wrists. Patch John whimpered as he sunk into the wet sheets and shivered.

My father had atrophy of the brain. As a result of his drinking, the tissues were swollen, making pressure in his head. After some weeks, the diagnosis was that Daddy would never be himself again, and the doctors at University Hospital were preparing to transfer him to Veteran's Hospital, where he would be a patient in the mental ward for the rest of his life.

Then a miracle happened. Walking down the hall, just a day before the transfer was to happen, he stopped in the doorway of a room where several physicians were in conference. A switch clicked on in his mind. He realized he was in a hospital and inquired how and when he had come there. A series of tests were run, the results indicating that he was rational and able to go home.

My telephone rang. I had been preparing for the worst. When I answered, I heard my father's voice explaining that he had suddenly found himself and would be coming to visit us. First, however, he planned to go to the reunion of his law school class. He sounded normal. How could that be?

As soon as he hung up, I called to verify what he had said. The doctor in charge of his case admitted flatly that he could not understand what had happened. By some miracle, my father had been given another chance. There was no medical explanation.

I looked at Patch John and then replied to the nurse, "Miracles have been known to happen."

If Patch John did get another chance, would he squander it like my father did, and return to drinking after only a year of grace?

Wolfman and Loose walked into the lobby as I was getting off the elevator. They were on their way up to see Patch John. They certainly were a scruffy duo!

Wolfman growled a "Good morning," Loose wiped his eyes, probably remembering times when I had come to see him at Harborview. I didn't stop for conversation. What was there to say?

I went straight from the hospital to the home of Jim, the retired architect from University Lutheran who lived in that neighborhood. The word "retirement" always made me smile when I thought of Jim. His lean, agile figure was always engaged in some useful project. Creativity exploded through his gray-haired cranium, spilling through his fingers into everything his 77-year-old imagination wished to change. Hour by hour, he spotted something, and plunged in with the urgency of a man who couldn't depend on tomorrow. Chances were that I would find him climbing on the hillside pruning one of his beloved rose bushes.

When the sun went down, he would begin transforming the interior of the house, designing a Buddhist alcove with treasures from Nepal or assembling a display of masks over the long staircase. Dramatic bursts of bold color accented the walls, providing backdrops for his valuable collections of Indian baskets, silver candleholders, hanging sculptures, and weavings. His home was a changing gallery. He got immense satisfaction in shifting his artifacts from space to space, catching visitors with surprises waiting behind the front door.

The surprise that morning was that he answered the bell between tasks. He ushered me to the patio and went to the kitchen for coffee. While it was only blocks from the hospital, it was "out of the city." I luxuriated in flowers and greens, as though transported back to a long-forgotten Eden. A bird with yellow feathers peered down from a branch, its head cocked in a question that I could not answer.

Jim reappeared, carrying a tray with scones, honey, butter, and fresh steaming coffee and cream.

"I just came from the hospital. Patch John is there in bad shape. I want to believe that he's going to get through this."

I paused, mulling the situation over in my mind.

"I wonder how many members feel the same. Are we doing the right thing, Jim? I mean, are we just enabling him to drink like our critics are saying? You are one of the few that keeps hanging in there. I have a question for you."

"What kind of question?" he asked as he poured coffee into mugs from Italy.

"Why? Why do you care about the boys on the porch?"

He wasn't expecting that question, but without hesitation he said something that surprised me. "My mother."

"You are a man in your seventies. Your firm designed the most prominent buildings in the city of Seattle. You have wealth, you are recognized in all of the important circles, travel the world, and are overflowing with energy and imagination. Others in the congregation walk by or dismiss or critique, but you get involved. Why? Mother was a long time ago."

"Mother was always doing something for someone. She left her impression. In the depression, bums would jump the freight trains and come to our back door. If they were hungry she fed them, no questions asked."

"You grew up on the Iron Range in northern Minnesota?" I asked, wanting to be sure I was remembering the story right.

"Yes. Interesting you should come with that question. There was another influence too. I'll be right back. I want to show you something I just found this morning in a box I was sorting." He flipped through the screen door, and reappeared almost in an instant.

He held a picture in his hand. In the center of it, an old man was holding a tiny black boy. The two of them were surrounded by children. Jim pointed to himself standing in the second row with an Indian on one side and a chubby blond Scandinavian boy on the other side. I wondered why there were no girls in the picture, but was even more puzzled to see four black faces.

"Who's the old man in the middle? And how did black kids get to a town way up there on the Iron Range?" I asked.

"We all called him Uncle Teddy, but he wasn't related to any of us. The blacks were there because of the work in the mines. Uncle Teddy never made distinctions, so neither did we. It might have been cold in winter and hot as hell in summer, but it was a good people climate to grow up in thanks to Mother and Uncle Teddy. It sticks with you somehow."

"What about your faith?" I really wanted to hear that the church had some influence.

"I went to Sunday School in that Lutheran church on the corner for hours and hours and hours. Some of that must have sunk into my soul," he said.

"I wonder why some people recognize each other and others remain complete strangers. You seem to know something about the boys that goes beyond surface judgment. Do you know what I am talking about?"

"No. Not really. I've never questioned or analyzed my involvement." His wiry body moved slightly in his chair. He never liked talking about his accomplishments.

It took me a few minutes to risk what was on my mind.

"Am I paying enough attention to the neighbors and some of our folks who are up to here with the whole thing? Is this wrong-headed? Am I naïve? Maybe we are just enabling the guys in their drinking."

"Of course we are enabling them! We're enabling them to live. We all have to be invited to live. That's what you said in one of your sermons," he replied.

"I'm always amazed when someone actually remembers something I said in a sermon. Apparently, I forget," I commented softly.

"You are having doubts," he stated.

"Doubts? No. I mean, yes. I question my own motives sometimes. Am I trying to be the Messiah and save the world? It is painful to see what's happening. We are running a hospice on our porch. Men are dying in the streets while we step over them on our way to important matters. But you stop to suffer through with them. And since I'm not Jesus, I need to be affirmed by the likes of you to hang in with the struggle."

"Now let me ask you a question. Why did they hang that stole around your neck when you got ordained?" Jim leaned forward, bringing his face closer to me.

"It's the yoke of servitude," I replied flippantly, giving the standard seminary answer.

"I don't know my Bible, according to chapter and verse, but there's something in there about yokes," he continued.

"Take my yoke and put it on you, and learn from me, because I am gentle and humble in spirit; and you will find rest. For the yoke I will give you is easy, and the load I will put on you is light," I recited from memory. Then, I paused for a moment, realizing in a fresh way what I had just said.

That yellow bird on the branch above suddenly flew away. It was as if both of us had gotten an answer to our questions, and now were free to go on.

* * * * *

Two members of the porch patrol, Joyce James, a registered nurse, and Mary Post, a retired social worker, faithfully reported their visits in the nightly log, which we kept hidden under the stairway.

After the second service one Sunday, they volunteered to take the altar flowers to Patch John, who had been hospitalized at Veterans Hospital for many weeks. Well- trained in medical matters, they fought the temptation to approach him as a case study instead of a fellow sinner in need of help. Geared to "fixing" people, their inclination was to pass judgment or prescribe alternate ways to cope with the severity of the problem. Love, faith, compassion, and a solid sense of obligation generally overshadowed their occupational instincts. I could certainly empathize with their frustrations with Patch John. When I arrived at his room, they were just leaving.

Joyce had tears in her eyes as she whispered, "Pastor June, I just experienced an unbelievable thing. Have you noticed an elderly man in the bed across from Patch John?"

Mary jumped into the conversation saying, "He is dying. His whole family has gathered around his bedside. He seems comfortable, but is barely conscious."

"Well," Joyce took over again, "we brought the flowers into the room and found John sitting in his bathrobe on top of his bed. He was surprised and visibly touched that we came. He has been drying out and looks much thinner. Anyway, we talked about church this morning, asked him how he was doing, got a vase and arranged the flowers, and were about to leave.

"He stood up, beckoned us to draw closer to him, and then said softly that the old man in the bed across from him needed some prayers. He invited us to join him in going over to the family," Mary continued.

"I couldn't believe it. Patch John went right up to the old man, took his hands, bowed his head, and began this beautiful prayer. Pastor June, he said the most simple, powerful words. It was like God's voice speaking to all of us through him. I felt a whole new sense of John. In fact, a whole new sense of the presence of God.

"When he finished the old man opened his eyes and smiled. His wife was crying and came right to John to hug him. She didn't say a word, but he resisted that same power to live his own life. What a waste!

"There he was, back on his bed. All I could see were his white-soled feet and his one brown eye. He was propped up on his pillows and smiled when he saw me enter the room. Before I could speak, his doctor hurried past me and went directly to him. Without any small talk, he got to the point.

"John, I wish I had better news for you. We got the results of your tests, and they are not good. Your liver has severe damage. One more bout of drinking will mean death. There are no more chances left. It is your choice. I can't help you anymore."

"He's heard this before, and he just keeps drinking. We've tried to tell him, but the message doesn't register," I said.

"Doctor, this is Pastor June. She's my minister," Patch John said. "Pastor June, would you pray with me?"

I was standing on one side of the bed and the doctor was standing on the other.

"No. Prayer goes two ways. You have to do your part. It is not magic. It is hard work," I said firmly, feeling at the end of my rope.

As I left, I heard Patch John tell his doctor, "I think she means it. I think she is mad at me."

Chapter Fifteen

THE UPPER ROOM

Fliers were tacked on telephone poles, taped on announcement boards in the grocery stores, and handed out up and down the Ave to invite people to a meeting in one of the restaurants. At the appointed time, the bartender was waiting at the door to point people upstairs to the lounge.

The owner of the place said runaways and panhandlers were clogging up his doorways, discouraging respectable paying customers. He asked the Chamber of Commerce to organize the meeting so some collective action could be taken to rid the Ave of vagrants. Monica Crystal, who worked for the Chamber, complied with his request. None of the boys was there. I didn't spot any of the other clergy there, either.

One side of the room was filled with clean-cut, middle-aged men in business suits. The other side was a rainbow of purple, orange, and gold hair, torn jeans, and snot-nosed babies on their mothers' shoulders. The room wasn't big enough. There was a sickening mix of cheap perfume, expensive cologne, body odors, and wet diapers. The guy next to me smelled of beer. There was no ventilation, and it was obvious that people were not comfortable touching bodies. Yet the crowd kept coming up the stairs and pushing their way into the meeting.

Crazy Mary, a familiar character on the Ave, was standing by the door. Her hair hung in snarled white rat's nests. She was agitated, shifting nervously from foot to foot while her eyes darted from floor board to floor board.

Three street kids shoved their way past her, and she let out a barrage of foul expletives. I recognized one of them from the teen shelter. His small white rat peeked over his collar, and I almost screamed. It was his pet and soon disappeared under his shirt. The businessmen stiffened and nodded at each other. It was time to get the meeting underway.

The owner of the establishment entered and took a spot at the front of the room. One of the babies started screaming. Her mother made no move to leave.

Crazy Mary shouted, "Stuff a tit in its mouth so we can hear, damn it!" it worked.

All eyes moved to the proprietor.

"I have invited you all to come to this open meeting so that we can reach some understanding about expectations here on the Ave," he began.

"Whose expectations?" the man with the beer breath asked.

"Will you just let me speak?" the owner responded defensively.

"Hell, we know what you want. You want us out of here. The sooner the better. Well, we ain't about to go nowhere. Sidewalks are public domain. This district is home to us. We live here. Just because we are out of work don't mean we aren't part of the community," the young mother said as she burped the baby on her shoulder.

Another businessman stepped forward. "If we have to close our shops and restaurants, there will be no community here for anyone. It used to be a very fashionable area of the city. Now, shoppers are afraid to come here."

"I was born and raised in the big house on the hill. My daddy was a wealthy man. Now I sleep in my car and my best friend is my dog. I am not out to hurt anyone. I'm a sick, old woman," Crazy Mary proclaimed.

No one took up with her. She was Crazy Mary: schizophrenic, weird, harmless. Her mental illness was treated as eccentricity. She lurked about in the alleys, curled up in the front seat of an old Cadillac at night, and haunted church offices during the day. In the evening, she picked out food from the trash bins behind the restaurants to feed her dog.

Just then, a police officer walked into the room.

"What are you doin' here, mister? We aren't breakin' no laws. We got our rights to assemble and speak out against injustice!"

The voice came from the back, in the corner. I couldn't see who spoke, but his comments drew a round of applause from the street people.

"The city council is enacting a new ordinance that prohibits you from panhandling and loitering on the streets. Anyone violating the law will be arrested and incarcerated," the officer announced.

"Look, your jails are bulging already. You don't have room for REAL criminals. Where are we going? How are we going to get through the courts? How are we going to pay fines? Give us some work, man! Give us a decent place to sleep!" It was the same voice, over in the corner.

"I don't make the rules. I just enforce them," the officer replied.

Tensions were rising. So were tempers. Innumerable blade-shaped mouths spit sharp-edged words across the room. The business community joined forces, yelling at the homeless, saying they had forced four establishments to declare bankruptcy within the past year.

One red-faced, purple-haired teen climbed up on a chair and shouted, "You bastards can't make it 'cause you just don't have imagination!" The rest of her crowd cheered.

"You tell 'em, Sadie. You tell 'em."

The proprietor declared the meeting over. It was amazing that nothing was broken and no one was injured. As I descended the steps, I spotted Emily, who was stepping up her campaign to run the boys off the porch.

The head of the Association for a Safer Saner Society (which the kids shortened to ASS, saying all its members were assholes) was chattering in her ear as she walked along toward the downstairs bar with Monica Crystal.

The three of them continued their discussion on bar stools, nursing tall, fluffy margaritas. I watched them for a few minutes, wondering if I should go over and talk to them. Instead, I went out the door with Crazy Mary, who turned and said, "Where are all the other preachers? Looking up chapter and verse someplace, eh?"

Before I could answer her, she slipped into the alley and disappeared into her car. Nobody was right. Nobody was wrong. We all staked our claim and tried to defend our place, including me. I was searching too, listening and testing out how to be in all of it.

I left that room to go to another upper room where I met with the Lord's disciples. Holy God in Heaven! I whispered in my deepest heart as I glanced around the circle at the people who volunteered to work on the porch patrol. There sat Jack Brigstone, a regional sales manager for a large insurance company; Martin King, an industrial engineer; Joyce James, a registered nurse who worked at Children's Hospital; Stan Cross, a researcher at Boeing; Mary Post, a retired counselor; Nancy Ward, a Lutheran deaconess; Cary Tangen, a travel agent; Beth Carsten, a professional mime; Maggie Frank, a seminarian; Grace Updown, graduate student; Jim Haney, architect; Clarence Pankowsky, an administrator at the University; and Bert Rhodes, our lay associate in ministry. Well-dressed, prosperous, educated professionals of high intelligence, they already worked overtime on their jobs. Some had small children. Why would they come back to the church late at night or in the early morning to monitor the porch?

In the beginning, there was much enthusiasm, but as the weeks went by, the numbers on the porch patrol dwindled. It was discouraging.

The boys continued to drink and pee and get sick on the steps. They were not easy to fix. The neighbors kept the pressure on. Discontent fermented among some of the other members. Good intentions gave way to other things that took priority on the agenda. Actions from City Hall gave no indication that tax dollars would be directed toward rehab or housing for the men, so our hope for more public responsibility was fading. We did not have the resources to carry on alone.

One Sunday morning after the coffee hour, Clarence Pankowsky asked to speak with me. He looked anxious and troubled. I finished greeting people, hung up my robes and met him in my office.

I closed the door and sat down on the couch across from him. Neither of us said anything. I patiently waited, sensing that he had to organize his thoughts.

"I have a confession to make," he began. "You'd never guess looking at me now that I lived on the streets, drank booze, and almost rotted away. I don't go to the porch out of compassion so much as out of duty. It's my duty to protect the premises. Every night I climb the steps, I take a lashing, not from them, but from my own self-disgust," he said, his voice breaking in anger.

He became strangely intoxicated with the remembrance of his own suffering and pain.

"Scolding them is taking revenge on the beast that has chewed me up for all the wasted years I spent in a stupor. Those guys make me sick! I have no pity for them. They are stray dogs poisoning themselves on the steps of MY church." The pitch got higher and the volume louder, as though somehow he could take power over the situation by elevating his voice. He calmed himself and continued.

"Then," he said, "one night, it became clear to me. I need to be forgiven and set free from the porch. I am the one who has to leave it behind. Too much of my own past is reappearing there, and until I can sift through the ashes, I can't purge my soul or theirs. I have too much unfinished business. I have been hiding my past and those guys are forcing me to see myself."

He studied my face, puzzling my reaction. His expression softened as though having just said it out loud, a weight had lifted from his heart.

He was asking for my permission to resign from the porch patrol. Together, we prayed for healing and freedom. He asked if I would continue to help him work out the spiritual dimensions of his experience. We made another appointment. When he left, I realized the core of the committed on the porch patrol was shrinking. There was no quick solution. Redemption wasn't cheap.

Chapter Sixteen

THE RUNAWAYS

The azalea bushes smelled so sweet in the spring air, I would have thought I was in a mountain meadow instead of on an urban thoroughfare. I was on my way to dinner, when that fragrance pulled me down, to take off my sweater and stretch out on the grassy lawn by the side of the church.

I thought of being four years old and going off with Franny Fridgen to the band concert in the park. Mother had the town policeman looking all over for us. I never understood why. We knew where we were. Franny and I were right there in the front row eating peanuts and listening to the music!

There must be a runaway in all of us, especially when the winter rains lift and all those months of wetness produce birds and flowers and wonderful green. What seemed so important inside the closed office now evaporated into intoxicating grace.

I became aware of voices on the porch. I must confess I eavesdropped as Champ started telling how he rode the boxcars. He had done a lot of that. One day, back in Rhode Island, he walked off his job, went to the railroad tracks, jumped onto a car and went to Florida. He didn't know why. He started living on the streets.

Then he met a fellow who hopped a freight train with him to Seattle. He met a nice woman. He married her. They were together for eight years and had two beautiful sons. But one day she got a truck, took the kids, moved everything out and left him. He couldn't handle it. Before long, he was back on the streets.

Drinking wasn't a problem for him, but self-esteem came hard. He claimed to be a slow learner, and it depressed him. All through grade school he had trouble reading. He fell behind and finally dropped out of school in the tenth grade. He couldn't concentrate very long on any one thing. He was restless. Gradually, I became restless too and picked myself up to go on to eat. Champ kept right on talking as he waved at me passing by.

The conversation that night was one of many that whetted the appetite for Wolfman and Ricco to persuade Champ to hop a train with them to Pasco, a town in eastern Washington, above the Oregon border, near Walla Walla. The three of them disappeared for months. Only Champ and Ricco returned. This is what Champ told us.

"Wolfman wore a forty-pound coat. His backpack was loaded with everything he owned. Now Wolfman had no notion about trains. He'd never been on one in his life, and certainly had never jumped from one. The train slides through Pasco at five miles an hour. It's not going to stop. Ricco and me knew that. We grabbed our gear and got ready to jump with the rhythm of the train. But Wolfman sat down, split his face open, and hit the rail. (Nobody ever went to get stitches. If they cut themselves, they just let it go. Probably the alcohol inside sterilized it.)

"He forgot to throw his loaded backpack off. I couldn't believe how he could run, being all sliced up and terrified like he was! He caught that train in less than four seconds, running alongside, and pulled his gear off from the edge. After all, it held everything he owned! But he had his fill of boxcars and he left us. We joined a carnival for the summer.

"I was in charge of the spiker," Champ continued. "It was a scary machine. Looked like an octopus except it only had one seat balanced on top of a pointed spike. Damn dangerous, it finally occurred to me. Ricco operated a game where you threw the ball four times for a dollar and if you hit the gong, got a white teddy bear. There was some way to fix it so the ball went off center, but Ricco never did that and he finally got fired.

"At the end of the season, a woman with big boobs and frizzy yellow hair come from eastern Washington someplace to take us to the next stop where the carnival was supposed to be. So we just climbed right into the van and fell asleep. When we woke up, we were almost in Las Vegas, the complete opposite way we were meant to go. She dropped us off in the desert.

"If it hadn't been for a policeman who came and rescued us, we would have died in that severe heat. There was something she wanted to get even with us about, but I never knew what that was. I was too damn mad to even think about it. Hitch by hitch, we got ourselves back to Seattle and the porch."

Champ didn't stay long after that. He got himself a place and didn't come out much. There was nothing out there that he cared for anymore. Somewhere a doctor gave him a ton of drugs that screwed him up and he said, "Stay away from me." Not that he wasn't witty and rational anymore. He just couldn't trust.

In his pocket, he carried pictures of his two sons. He flashed them with pride. Ever since they came to see him on the streets, their mother forbade them to come again. Even when he got a place, she refused to allow for them to see him. Lonely, he kept to himself. Only now and then, he would set up a meeting with his friends from the porch or stop in at my office for an update.

He'd talk about the days they sat by the Safeway store, down the hill from the church. He refused to say he begged. Some people were ugly. They kicked as they walked past, or called out insults. He got so used to it, he turned numb. He knew they didn't understand up there what was going on beneath them. He had to believe there was good in people. He had to forgive and expect decency.

And there were decent people. Lots of them, who stopped to talk, who expressed concern, who even dropped a coin or a bill for the next meal. They kept him alive in body and spirit. Otherwise, he said we would not have been able to live on the sidewalk. Now, with a little money from some jobs he had, and his Social Security checks, he had a place where nobody could insult him or call him names.

Nobody came to the porch without bringing something along. It was true of the new guy who volunteered to make the rounds with Bert. Not only did he have a squad of rebellious teenagers at home, he had been trained to go into conflict situations with rescue crews and firemen where it didn't pay to take chances. His brain was educated to react. In emergencies, his cheeks flushed and his eyes glinted in anticipation of danger. Though not consciously, his body instinctively readied for battle whenever he was on assignment.

Something unfortunate happened because of that. Wolfman was sitting in Hope's office waiting for me. It was exceptional that he would risk coming to talk by himself, since he was a follower, not a leader. I invited him into my office, and told Hope to hold calls.

I didn't have to invite him to speak. He no sooner sat down than he burst into tears and blurted out, "It's so damn unfair."

"What's unfair, Wolfman?" I asked.

"That the kid should get the handcuffs instead of the big brute that kicked him."

"I'm lost. Back up a little. What kid? What brute?" I had no idea what he was talking about.

"This morning. Some teenager with a bicycle pulled in under the stairwell by the Fellowship Hall. I seen him come in around 4:00 a.m. He was really wiped out. He biked up from Portland. Anyway, about 8:00 a.m. Bert ... I know him ... and this other guy I never seen before, climb all over us shouting that we have to get up and move out because there's some school starting."

"Vacation Bible School," I explained.

"Whatever. They were comin' on real pushy and bossy like. Some of us regulars didn't give 'em no grief. We just started getting our things together, ready to head down the hill. But they came back a second time and the kid with the bike was dead asleep. So, the new guy."

"The brute, as you call him?" I interrupted.

"Yeah, I seen him go up and kick the kid and yell at him. Anybody on the streets who is waked up so rough like that is goin' to protect himself. That's the law of the jungle! He jumped up and started slugging. The kid pushed the guy's glasses off his face. The big guy kicked him again and put him in a head lock. He held him down and pretty soon, the kid pulled a knife out of his pocket. Bert ran into the office to call the police. The big guy backed off, but wouldn't let the kid run.

"When the cops came, they believed the big guy, who is a member of your congregation. He was looking for his glasses as they walked up. The kid had ditched the knife. He looked scared. The kid said he had no parents or relatives around here. The cops frisked him, treated his bruises, and he tried to tell them his side of the story, but they snapped the cuffs on him and took him away in the police car. I'm tellin' you the truth, Pastor June. That kid shouldn't take the rap for this. He was the one who was attacked!"

"I believe you. It was good you told me. Thank you. I'll follow up and see what I can do."

Where to start, who to talk to first? I decided to go to the police station. When I arrived, I discovered "the brute" had already been there with a contrite heart. He dropped any charge and told the officers that he had provoked the incident. The kid left on his bike to go north to Vancouver.

But that wasn't the end of it. Bert took it along to the next council meeting when I was out of town at a conference. Apparently, when the police came that morning, they convinced him that the church was too vulnerable, having strays sleeping on the property.

Bert was a peaceful fellow who nurtured his interior space with meditation, spiritual direction, art, and theology. Evil and violence unnerved his soul. Going to the porch caused uneasy feelings that challenged him sometimes beyond his capacity to cope. He got headaches and spasms in his neck from the stress. He had a diminutive frame, a balding head, and a slight stoop in his shoulders. Perhaps it was because he carried so much on his own back. Encounters made him feel weak and ineffectual, maybe even cowardly. He wished the whole scene would disappear. He recommended that the council authorize that the building be posted with criminal trespass signs and that the police be permitted to use their uniform to do most of the work. The motion passed unanimously.

When I returned and got the council's decision, all I could hear was a sugary sweet voice saying, "Wonderful! So it is all taken care of then."

I heard arguments that there was a different class of people coming to the district. Needles and condoms were found under the bushes. (Some of them left by university students on their way up the hill past the property, I suspected.) The key argument was the recent incident with the knife, which for many finally illustrated how dangerous conditions were becoming.

People had forgotten how threatened they were when the boys first showed up in the neighborhood with their hairy faces, disgusting toilet habits, and lack of social grace. They had not registered that the hard times worked miracles in everyone.

I knew that many had been changed on that porch. Not only the men, but the ones who came to meet them there. I felt strongly that the new wave of visitors was no more intimidating than others had been. It was that the small core on the porch patrol was weary and disappointed. Their threshold for acceptance was worn down, and they were searching for a legitimate reason to quit. Conventional wisdom prevailed.

It reminded me of a story. One weekend, a family who had for generations lived on the same farm, received a visit from their first cousin's son, a graduate student majoring in botany at the University. They seldom had company, had lost touch with the rest of the family, and were both excited and wary of his coming... He arrived late Friday evening.

Early the next morning, he took a walk into the farmyard and saw a patch of berries by the barn. He got a bowl from the kitchen and filled it with juicy, plump blueberries as his surprise contribution for breakfast.

The family was surprised. They asked him where he had found them and he was quick to reply, "Out by the barn."

"Oh, no!" the father protested. "We never pick those. They are not safe to eat."

"Of course they are safe to eat," the young guest laughed.

He impressed them with the botanical name of the plant, poured cream over them and ate them before their very eyes. They watched in horror, as spoon by spoon, he continued eating until he emptied the bowl.

The next morning, the same thing happened. The family anxiously exchanged glances waiting to see the consequences of his indulgence in spite of their warnings. Again, he showed no signs of sickness, poisoning or strange behavior.

Sensing something was wrong, the young man asked as he was leaving if he had upset them.

The farmer hesitated, not wanting to challenge a learned relative, "Those berries you brought in. They are forbidden. You can die if you eat those."

The young man said, "Don't you see that I am well? Those berries are safe and perfectly delicious. You should enjoy them!"

That night, after the visitor had gone back to the city, the farmer uprooted all the berry bushes and burned them.

When we are grounded in a belief system, it is hard to undo it—especially when it is rooted in the cultural circles that have been part of our survival and development.

Chapter Seventeen

AMAZING GRACE

I did not go back to Patch John. It had been months since I walked away from him. He had left the hospital, and one day he called me.

"I heard you were asking around about me, but I didn't want to be in touch until I knew I was on the way. You were so mad at me. It really shook me up, Pastor June. Somethin' snapped when you walked out on me. I think your not praying with me scared me. It was like I felt ashamed to be teasing God with prayers I didn't want answered. You know? Praying to get sober while I was lathering for my next drink? All the time, you kept telling me that I was worth something, that you believed I could be more than I was. When you went out, I looked at the flowers from the church and figured the next bouquet would be for my funeral."

After his release, he went to help other recovering alcoholics who frequented an outreach program in a Baptist church in a section of Seattle called Capitol Hill. He was part of a staff, earning a paycheck, and doing something for other people. He had his own living quarters, a telephone, and a kitchen where he could cook his own food. But his best news was that he had been sober for almost eight months.

"Patch John! This is unbelievable. I gave up, but you didn't!"

"Could you come over to see where I work?" he asked.

"I know right where that church is. I'll be there tomorrow afternoon," I promised.

He was wearing a short-sleeved, white shirt, open at the neck, and over it a black vest, neatly buttoned, that matched his pressed black trousers. His face was clean-shaven, except for a finely trimmed mustache. He stood tall and proud in the threshold of the street entrance to the church basement. The patch was gone. He had put on weight, not much, just enough to fill his frame. It was strange seeing him without the patch. The Veteran's Administration fixed him up with an artificial eye. It gave him the Sammy Davis, Jr. look.

"How are you, Pastor June?" he greeted me in his usual soft-spoken voice.

"Hey! Don't I get a hug?" I burst upon him.

Suddenly, I felt embraced in the strong arms of a man who had recovered his dignity. I was sure that he had forgotten much that happened during those days on the porch. As we tried to reflect together, he frankly confessed that all that concerned him then was where his next drink could be found.

Once he achieved sobriety, he recognized his reluctance to get treatment came from a dread of facing the responsibility of life in a conscious world. He was without hope until he admitted that he needed help. Once he got it, he turned his life toward others who were not yet liberated.

I wondered if the congregation would come to understand their reluctance to face that same dread: the dread of facing the responsibility and pain that comes in emerging from the dreamlike fog we float through as middle-class Americans.

We stood by the door engaged in deep conversation, until he finally invited me into the downstairs of the church where he assisted in the outreach program five days a week. There was new green carpet on the floor and fresh paint on the pillars and walls. The atmosphere was encouraging and bright.

"There is someone else here who wants to see you," Patch John announced with a wide grin. We walked into another room.

I had no idea who the man was who sat on the sofa strumming the strings of the guitar in his lap.

"Pastor June?" he looked up from beneath the brim of his leather hat.

"I am sorry. Am I supposed to know you?" I was genuinely puzzled.

"It's Loose. Don't you recognize him?" John asked.

"Loose? You are Loose? Someone told me you died. I cried a bucket over you, you scoundrel." I stood dumbfounded.

"You might say I did die. Come here. Sit down. Let me tell you what happened."

I sat by him, trying to digest what I was experiencing.

"I feel like I'm sitting with Lazarus. You were a rotten piece of flesh the last time I saw you. Yellow and shaking, with blurry eyes. You couldn't put one foot in front of the other, and your tongue spit bitter venom," I stated candidly.

"I was pretty bad, wasn't I?" He started picking out *Why Don't You Come Home, Bill Bailey?* on the guitar.

"So, you really do play that thing?" I asked, surprised again. "Keep playing."

I stretched out, closed my eyes, and listened. He switched tunes to *Amazing Grace*. It reminded me of the memorial service in the park.

I was lifted to a high peak.

Patrick appeared before me, dressed in white cloth.

Lenny stood beside him. They had stopped their wanderings. The clouds that enveloped them were not the fuzzy overhangs of alcoholic blur, but shrouds of mystery and pure light. There was an empty chair. Bamboo huts that looked like fruit stands were filled with grapes fresh-picked from the vineyards. A fire burned nearby. We were on a mountain, and the chill of evening was beginning to settle. They did not see me, even though I could see them plainly. When I called to them, they suddenly disappeared.

Jesus was now sitting in the chair. He extended a cup of the new wine to me and then a veil fell over his brilliant face.

Loose swung into a spirited tempo that jolted me from the vision. When I sat up, he stopped playing and began telling his story.

"The medics picked me up down on the Ave, I guess. I shouldn't have lived, according to what I was told. That was a long time ago, it feels like now. I woke up one day in the hospital with a circle of doctors in white coats telling me about all the things that had gone wrong. They said I wasn't gonna get no better, but I didn't have to get lots worse.

"I left there for a rehab place and then a kind of a vista rest home situation. I dried out without all the withdrawal and tough stuff Patch went through. Hard to believe, but I got more humble. For years on the street, I'd heard testimonies and read a lot of Bible scripture, but none of that pertained to my life. I just didn't see the views of it. In fact, I got pretty sarcastic and hostile.

"Not drinking, I got to realize how much idle time I had. I wanted to make it more productive. I saw action from asking for something, so I asked. I'd never experienced the kind of feeling that came. It just hit me like a bolt, real quick. It didn't hurt me. I don't know how to say it, except I got a new life. It was like something fell away from my eyes and I was real aware of it. I felt frightened for about fifteen seconds. I thought I was having another crazy spell, but it was something more lasting than an episode.

"I haven't had a drop to drink in all these days, and I picked up my guitar and started singing again. I'm not having conversations about death anymore. I'm talkin' about life and glad to be living it. I met Him. That's the only reason I can give for my sobriety."

Patch John joined the testimony.

"As cold as that porch got some nights, and as cloudy as my mind was, I got little shocks of warm love every time God's people stopped to check me out," Patch John said. "I stuffed that deep down somewhere and the message got buried for a time. But when I had to have it, it rose up like thunder and I heard my name spoken like I was a real man. A person of credit. Somebody was telling me I was worth something, and I got to believing it!"

We all laughed. We had lost each other, and now we were found.

So many pilgrims traveled immeasurable distances while standing on the same corner.

Deep within us, there is planted the warning to avoid those who are unfamiliar to us, who come from outside, especially if they speak with the voice of illness.

Yet, inevitably, the laws of our common biological existence will bring us face to face.

In the book of Revelations, we are given the vision of the city of God. There the ill are included, respected and regarded as fully human.

It is a city for the healing of the nations where the streets begin to flow with kindness and relief. We are sent as healers to touch the wounds, repair the hatred and mend the tears that rip the fabric of our lives.

We have but one assignment: *To love our neighbors.*

AFTERWORD

by Reverend Ron Moe-Lobeda
Pastor, University Lutheran Church
Seattle, Washington

Building on the experience of the Porch Patrol in the mid-1990s, members of University Lutheran Church (ULC) decided in 2000 to use their entire church facility in a way that was more consistent with their mission. After a year of discernment, they chose to establish a ministry with homeless women at ULC, formed a separate corporation to govern this new organization, and named it Elizabeth Gregory Home (EGH).

At the same time, members of ULC and Christ Episcopal Church in the University District established the Sanctuary Art Center (SAC)—a program that welcomed homeless young people into a calm space at ULC for the purpose of developing their artistic talent.

In 2009, ULC responded to a request by a local organization that managed emergency shelters and decided to host the University Lutheran Women's Shelter for up to 15 women every night of the year. About that same time, ULC doubled its commitment to Teen Feed and decided to host this program for homeless young people twice a week. With these four programs in place, ULC has become a safe refuge of hospitality for homeless young people and women of all ages.

At the EGH Day Center, more than 30 women a day enter the doors of ULC and have access to hot meals, laundry facilities, computers, a clothing closet, a food bank, a place to rest, and, most importantly, a compassionate staff and corps of volunteers to assist them in their next step of securing a job, furthering their education, or getting a key to a permanent home of their own.

Currently, plans are in place to double the size of the Day Center by renovating space for a Wellness Center, which will include two accessible showers for the women—a much-needed amenity for homeless women. EGH also operates a transitional home near ULC for eight women who live in community and have a stable place to live while getting back on their feet.

The homeless young people flock to the SAC at ULC five days a week to engage in many forms of art—painting, making pottery, playing music, acting, and designing murals. One room at ULC is set up with two T-shirt printing machines, which the SAC uses to train a few of these young people as interns in the art of designing and printing T-shirts. Thousands of T-shirts are shipped in and out of ULC each year, as this enterprise generates income for the SAC and allows this organization to accommodate more and more young people in this quiet spiritual refuge at ULC.

The heart of ULC continues to be one of worship and hospitality. As the members of ULC are received at the table by Jesus and invited to share in his holy meal, they have responded by opening up their facility to those who are most vulnerable in our community and welcoming them into this holy place. ULC has become the face and place of love in the community and a shining example of what it means to love our neighbors.

DISCUSSION QUESTIONS

1. What is the most inspirational message you are taking away from reading this book?

2. What are the identifying characteristics of what it is to be human? Where did you find examples of that in this book?

3. Why is it so difficult to love our neighbors?

4. Can you remember an incident in which you overcame fear and were transformed in a relationship?

5. Are you helping to facilitate a social shift?

6. To which of the characters in this story were you most attracted? Why?

7. To which of the characters did you have a hard time relating? Why?

8. What is being done to address homelessness in your community?

ACKNOWLEDGMENTS

My deep appreciation to:

Elizabeth Gregory, whose strong Spirit and vision inspired the congregation to spearhead actions to assist homeless women, even as she herself faced terminal cancer.

Pastor Ron Moe-Lobeda, whose wisdom and good judgment has guided the congregation and wider community to actualize even more than thought possible. All in God's time and order, we accomplish Spirit's plans.

Kira Henschel, my publisher, whose counsel, personal commitment, and professional experience made this a co-creative process. Besides all that, I really love her warmth and integrity.

The Porch Patrol, the staff and church council who put themselves on the line. One of them once said, " Of course. That's what Christians do."

ABOUT THE AUTHOR

I n 1970, when the Lutheran Church in America approved the ordination of women, June Nilssen Eastvold was among the first to be ordained. During her forty years of ordained ministry, she has served on the Commission of 70, elected to design the newly formed Evangelical Lutheran Church in America (ELCA). She served as Lutheran campus pastor at the University of Wisconsin-Milwaukee, where she founded the Gamaliel Chair for Peace and Justice. In addition, she attended the 1996 United Nations International Conference for Women in Beijing, China, and has gone on mission trips to El Salvador, Nicaragua, Senegal, South Africa, Greece, and Mexico.

The Boys on the Porch is based on her years as an activist in Seattle, Washington, while serving in the university district as the pastor at University Lutheran Church.

June is married to Michael Frome, noted author and conservationist. They live in Port Washington, Wisconsin, in a tree house above Lake Michigan. She is the mother of three grown children and has three grand-daughters.

June Eastvold can be reached through the publisher at info@henschelHAUSbooks.com

AN EASTER NOTICE

Dear Members of the Congregation of the University Lutheran Church (ULC):

The neighbors of your church are distributing this note with the hope that as a congregation you can influence the course of action that your pastor is following. The single family home owners and others have tried to reason with the ULC leadership, without success.

The situation has deteriorated to the extent that the University District Community Council (UDCC) is requesting city enforcement for a public health menace.

This is what we face on a daily basis:

1. Drunken men are sleeping on the church steps, porches, and in the bushes. They urinate, defecate, and vomit on the church grounds. Their litter is empty wine bottles, trash, and used toilet paper. We have taken one hypodermic needle from the steps near the curb on 16th NE. We have photos for documentation.

2. The men have begun going into neighborhood yards to relieve themselves.

3. The men have harassed children and adults.

4. Most recently, a man was observed masturbating during the day by one of the preschool teachers.

In January, a letter from the church was written to the neighborhood that distorted the facts. The number of sleeping and drunk men, and the amount of filth outside of the church is steadily increasing despite the claim to the opposite.

The church's neighbors should not be its victims. It is **misguided** Christian charity which condones the activities listed above. **Real** Christian charity would provide drug rehabilitation, a proper facility, supervision, and indoor toilets. Please, please call your ULC council members and tell them that you do **not** want your church to be this neighborhood's cesspool.

Thank you.

The Sorensens   The Thomases
The Fercher
Also Kelly & Joe

The Baumakins
The Melveys
The Gallucci's
The Flemings

Original of letter responding to the Easter Notice
presented on page 118.

NIVERSITY LUTHERAN CHURCH

1604 Northeast Fiftieth Street, Seattle, Washington 98105
Phone 525-7074

April 14, 1993

Dear Neighbors and Members of University Lutheran:

Over the past months we have provided a temporary sanctuary for a few men who have come looking for a peaceful place. They are alcoholics. They are in need of all the things you listed in the leaflet distributed on Easter Sunday (see back). The city is not providing adequate safe shelter, treatment, or a clear invitation to recovery. Once rehabilitated there are no jobs, no housing, no encouragement.

There are people in the building from early morning to around 10 PM each night. No one has complained about a "cesspool". Our grounds are kept well. Our porch is closely monitored. It is our property. Teams of our members have faithfully gone to the porch. We have kept a log and monitored alcohol use, condition of the porch, and general behavior. When our visitors have become sick on our place, we have taken the responsibility to clean up.

Nothing would indicate that the needle you referred to belonged to the men on our porch. Hundreds of people pass by our corner. We are across the street from the squat which the police raided recently, not far from fraternity row, and only a few blocks above the Ave.

No report was filed with us by the daycare that a man was masturbating in front of their staff member. None of us has witnessed such behavior. Should that occur on our property we would, of course, address the problem.

It is our hope that your letter indicates concern, not just about our small effort to meet human need, but about a growing awareness of the critical nature of the social changes that are happening in the district.

We will join you in your community efforts to provide rehabilitation, a proper facility, supervision and indoor toilets. We admit that our efforts are inadequate and would welcome a combined cooperative effort that invites all segments of the University District to find humane, just solutions to these difficult situations.

The sooner we come up with alternatives, the sooner our porch people will move.

Members of The University Lutheran Church Council,
Douglas Miller, Council Chair
Pastor June Nilssen, Congregational President
Jeanne Rehwinkel, Social Ministry Chair
Marshall Pihl, Property Chair

Rev. June Eastvold Nilssen, Pastor

Rev. Olin Dasher, Visitation Pastor   Allen Roehl, Associate in Mini

CPSIA information can be obtained at www.ICGtesting.com
Printed in the USA
LVOW07s1819020115

421245LV00005B/10/P

9 781595 983381